Also in this series:

ECUMENICAL STUDIES IN WORSHIP

No. 15

THE WORSHIP OF
THE REFORMED CHURCH

An Exposition and Critical Analysis of the Eucharistic, Baptismal,
and Confirmation rites in the Scottish, English-Welsh, and Irish
liturgies

by

JOHN M. BARKLEY, M.A., Ph.D., D.D.

JOHN KNOX PRESS

Richmond, Virginia

ECUMENICAL STUDIES IN WORSHIP

General Editors:

CONTENTS

Published by Lutterworth Press, London, England, 1966,
and John Knox Press, Richmond, Virginia, 1967.

I

INTRODUCTION

"I," SAID A Scottish Divine, "am first a Christian; secondly, a Catholic; thirdly, a Calvinist; fourthly, a Paedo-baptist; and, fifthly, a Presbyterian."[1]

When discussing the Reformed Church, which, owing to the controversy over Church-Order in the sixteenth and seventeenth centuries, in English-speaking countries is commonly called the Presbyterian Church, it is important to stress that to be Reformed or Presbyterian it is essential to be Christian, Catholic, Calvinist, and Paedo-baptist. This applies not only to doctrine, but to worship.

In the Reformed Church all worship is centred in the person and work of Jesus Christ, His incarnation and life, teaching, death, resurrection and ascension. What is done is done "in the name and by the authority of Jesus Christ". Worship must be Christian.

All Reformed Service-Books and Hymnals draw upon the devotional heritage of Christendom. In this sense, Reformed rites are Catholic. Yet this is not sufficient to give full expression to Catholicity, because to do so requires that the rites be structured and ordered in harmony with Catholic practice. They, also, should be linked to the Christian Year.

To speak of Reformed worship as Calvinistic is to run the risk of being misunderstood, because there is so much misrepresentation of Calvinism.

Christian worship rests upon a doctrinal basis, and ultimately upon the Christian doctrine of God. We do not worship a Supreme Being or an Unknown God, but One whose nature and character have been revealed to us. What, therefore, we say and do in worship must be adjusted to the doctrine of God. Worship must not be regarded as other than adoration of God as He has made himself known (in Jesus Christ through the Holy Spirit) to His Church.[2]

[1] Quoted R. Parke, *Presbyterianism*, n.d., p. 1.
[2] R. E. Parsons (ed.), *Worship and Education*, 1939, p. 20. Words in brackets added by writer.

7

If one remembers, making due allowance for "scruples" in particulars, that the fundamental doctrine of Calvinism is the absolute sovereignty of God, it is certainly correct to say that Reformed worship must be Calvinist.

To speak of Reformed worship as Paedo-baptist does not mean that it is sufficient for a Service-Book to contain a rite for the baptism of the infant children of believers. Much more is involved, in that the doctrine of the Church must be one which holds the visible church to consist "of all those throughout the world that profess the true religion, together with their children";[1] a doctrine of marriage that holds every aspect of the union to be "in the Lord"; and a doctrine of God who is a Covenant God.

Only when expression is given to these essentials may worship be considered Reformed or Presbyterian. Leaving aside, for the moment, the Ordinal and traditional practices (for example, singing metrical psalms), let us try to understand what is meant by Reformed or Presbyterian. We have seen that worship is based on doctrine. There are three distinct classes of doctrines (i) Catholic doctrines, common to all Christians, which are summarized in the Apostles' Creed and the Nicene; (ii) Evangelical doctrines, common to all Protestants, by which they are distinguished from Roman Catholics; and (iii) Particular doctrines, which are distinctive of the individual churches; for example, the Reformed are distinguished from Lutherans principally in their doctrine of the sacraments, and from Arminians in their doctrine of grace and salvation.[2] To speak of worship as Reformed means that as well as giving expression to Catholic and Evangelical doctrine it must also be in harmony with the distinctive doctrines of the Reformed Church.

The distinctive characteristic of Christian worship is, as we have seen, that it is "in the name of Jesus Christ". He has revealed God to us. But this is not all. Christian worship is not simply the experience of an individual, but of the individual in community. It is the worship of a family, the church.

Three vital points arise out of this: (i) Because worship expresses our faith in God it must consist of adoration and thanksgiving, humility and repentance, learning from God, prayer for others and for ourselves; (ii) Worship is always corporate; even when a Christian is praying alone he is nevertheless praying with other Christians and with the

---

[1] *Westminster Confession of Faith*, 25: 2 (hereafter referred to as WCF).

[2] J. M. Barkley, *Westminster Formularies in Irish Presbyterianism*, 1956, p. 14.

Church; and (iii) Because worship is corporate, it is always outward as well as inward, and thus uses words and silence, music and action, light and colour, and so on.

We must now outline briefly the origins of Christian worship and of the Reformed rites.

II

THE REFORMED RITE ON THE CONTINENT

WHEN ONE speaks of the Liturgy, it must be remembered that one speaks of a living organism, for, as Professor R. Will says, "Certainly form without spirit is dead, but spirit without form is not capable of living."[1] Dr. Streeter, also, reminds us that, "No new or revised 'Order of Service' can be the best, or can be even tolerably good, unless it is organically related to and a natural development of the custom and practice of the past."[2] Thus it is necessary to refer briefly to the worship of the early church.

Jesus and his disciples were Jews; consequently Judaism influenced greatly the forms of worship in the early church. Jewish worship had three centres: the Temple, the synagogue and religious meals. The first of these did not exert any great influence in the early church except in the sphere of psalmody. On the other hand, the influence of the other two was, as we shall see, very far-reaching.

The evangelists tell how our Lord regularly took part in the worship of the synagogue.[3] St. Luke informs us that this was also the practice of the apostles.[4] The early Christians naturally made use of the synagogue forms of worship in their own meetings. Synagogue worship consisted in reading from the Old Testament (Law and Prophets) with exposition, praise and prayer. These four elements continued in Christian worship, but they were permeated with a new meaning and spirit. Praise and prayer were "in the name of Christ", and to the Old Testament readings were added gradually readings from the Epistles and Gospels.

One point requires to be mentioned, namely, the position of the prayers. "Rabbinic scholars are in disagreement as to whether the prayers came first or last in the synagogue of the first century A.D. . . . In the third century the Jews undoubtedly placed them in a group at the beginning. . . . But in all Christian Churches from the earliest

---

[1] R. Will, *Le Culte*, 1925, ii, 31.
[2] B. H. Streeter, *Concerning Prayer*, 1916, p. 290.
[3] Mark 1: 21–28; 3: 1–5; 6: 1–6; Luke 4: 15–32.
[4] Acts 9: 20–22; 13: 5, 14–44; 14: 1–4; 17; 1–4, 16–17; 18: 4–11, 24–28.

moment . . . the prayers were universally placed last, after the sermon."[1] Instruction in the scriptures led to prayer.

Religious meals were common in Judaism, and Jesus met with His disciples for many such meals. It is uncertain whether the Last Supper Jesus had with His disciples was the Passover meal,[2] or a meal in preparation for the Passover.[3] It does not greatly matter, for the Passover was a season, rather than a meal, so the Passover would be in the mind of Jesus and His followers. At this meal Jesus took bread, gave thanks, and brake it, saying, "This is my body which is for you"; and He took the Cup of Blessing, and gave thanks, saying, "This cup is the new covenant in my blood."[4] It was natural that Jesus' action should be interpreted in terms of His life, death and resurrection. In its celebration Christians meet with and are united to their risen Lord, and through Him are united to one another.[5] It appears certain that from the very first Christians met together on the first day of each week for this festival of the Breaking of Bread.[6]

In the earliest days of Christianity, as in modern mission-fields and new housing estates, worship was frequently conducted in private houses,[7] or, as did the Jews where they had no synagogue, at a special place for prayer, often situated by the river side.[8] Later, special buildings were erected for worship and their structure resembled the civil basilica in the Roman Empire.[9] This began early in the fourth century when Christianity ceased to be an illegal cult.

From the Sacred Year of the Jews originated the concept of the Christian Year. The first great Christian festival to be observed was Easter Day. Later, Holy Week was added, to be followed by Pentecost, Epiphany and Christmas. Later, festivals of the saints, at first observed only locally, were added.

Justin Martyr,[10] writing about A.D. 155, gives an account of Christian worship, which shows how from the first the following elements were preserved:

---

[1] G. Dix, *The Shape of the Liturgy*, 1945, p. 37.
[2] Mark 14: 12.
[3] John 18: 28; 19: 14.
[4] Matthew 26: 26–29; Mark 14: 22–25; Luke 22: 19–20; I Cor. 11: 23–26.
[5] I Cor. 10: 14–17.
[6] Acts 20: 7.
[7] Acts 18: 7; 19: 9; 20: 7–8; Rom. 16: 5; Col. 4: 15; Philemon 2.
[8] Acts 16: 13.
[9] J. W. Crowfoot, *Early Churches in Palestine*, 1941, p. 48.
[10] Justin, *Apology*, i, 65, 67.

Reading of Scripture
Sermon
Prayers for all men
Offering (a) gifts for the needy
(b) bread and wine for the Eucharist
Prayer of Thanksgiving by the "President", the people responding, Amen
Distribution to those present by the "President", and taken to the absent by deacons.

It will be seen that the first three are based on the worship of the synagogue, and the others on the Last Supper.

Since the publication of Dix, *The Shape of the Liturgy*, it has become customary to speak of the fourfold shape of the eucharistic rite—Offertory, Consecration, Manual actions, and Communion.[1] This has been challenged, and rightly so, by Professor J. G. Davies, as an oversimplification.[2] The entire action of the Eucharist must be seen as one and indivisible—a unity—the one action having four elements, all of which are closely linked and interrelated.

This common form has been elaborated in different ways in the East and West, though the main outline remains the same. The additions divide principally into four groups:

(a) an introduction of praise and prayer in the form of a preparation before the Readings from Scripture;
(b) the introduction of the Creed after the prayers for all men;
(c) the incorporation of additional elements into the Anaphora;[3] and
(d) the addition of a conclusion of prayer and praise after the partaking.

When one examines the New Testament writings and those of the early fathers, there appear to be six distinctive elements or aspects[4] in the Service:

(i) It is a festival of thanksgiving;
(ii) It is a festival of fellowship with Christ and with one another in Him;
(iii) It is a festival of commemoration, on the historical side;

---

[1] G. Dix, *op. cit.*, p. 50.
[2] *Parish and People*, 1958, pp. 3 ff.
[3] Hippolytus, *Apostolic Tradition; Liturgy of St. James.*
[4] Y. Brilioth, *Eucharistic Faith and Practice*, 1934; O. Cullmann, *Essays on the Lord's Supper*, 1958.

(iv) It is a festival of sacrifice, including Christ's "once for all" offering of Himself for us, and the church's self-oblation;

(v) It is a festival of resurrection, Christ is alive and present; and

(vi) It is a festival of holy mystery.

In the eucharistic rite these six elements ought to be held in proper balance, but if one is exalted at the expense of the others the meaning of the rite suffers distortion. This happened in the Western Church in the Middle Ages. The other aspects of the rite were "over-shadowed by the offering of the sacrifice".[1] Because of this, because of other doctrinal distortions, and because of the fact that worship was conducted in the Latin language, which many of the faithful did not understand, the Reformers had to face the problem of public worship. Their principal sources of knowledge were the New Testament, patristic evidence (non-liturgical, for the most part), and the Roman Missal. Their purpose was to make the church a worshipping community. They sought to make worship CORPORATE and ACTIVE. It was to be the corporate action of the people of God, not something done on their behalf; and something done not by individuals but together.

The use of the vernacular was a necessity, if all were to understand and intelligently to participate in the public worship of God. This was recognized by all, but many hesitated to take the step involved in such a drastic uprooting of tradition. However, the step was eventually taken, and our interest lies principally in the reforms in Strasbourg, Geneva, Frankfurt, and Scotland.

The first revision of the Mass in Strasbourg was made by Diebold Schwarz, who before he joined the reforming party had been a Dominican and a Brother of the Order of the Holy Spirit. It was he, who on February 16, 1524, first celebrated Mass in German in St. John's Chapel in the Cathedral at Strasbourg. It was based on the Hagenau Missal,[2] and was an almost literal translation into German of the mediaeval mass. While as much as possible of the old familiar ritual was retained, his approach was creative rather than negative, and by slight omissions and by paraphrasing, the spirit of the Reformers was adequately expressed and the best feature of the old service retained. Concerning this rite, Dr. W. D. Maxwell writes, "Evangelical in spirit, but Catholic in form, it is the bridge between the more definitely Protestant worship of the later Reformed Church and the

[1] Y. Brilioth, op. cit., p. 82.

[2] J. Smend, Die evangelischen deutschen Messen bis zu Luthers deutscher Messe, 1896, p. 146.

mediaeval ceremonialism of the Roman Church."[1] While much of the old ceremonial is retained and the service is a translation of the Roman Mass, there was a purifying of the doctrinal basis of the rite; for example, the Roman doctrine of sacrifice is expurgated and also all invocations of the Virgin and the saints.

Schwarz made five changes which, because they are constructive, should not pass unrecognized. Firstly, the doctrinal basis underlying the rite was changed towards the Reformed position. Secondly, the rite was to be said audibly and in the vernacular, which resulted in the fact that, although much of the traditional ceremonial remained, the people were not dependent upon it to follow the service. Thirdly, he restored the communion of the people in both kinds. Fourthly, the *Confiteor*, formerly said by the priest, was slightly modified and enlarged, and was to be said aloud as a general confession of the people though the use of the first person singular was retained. And, fifthly, his treatment of the Canon of the Mass was constructive. While he simplified its form without altering its essential character, the Canon was retained and continued to be entitled as such.

A further five editions were issued in 1524. There is still no sermon, and the principal changes are a reduction in ceremonial, and the provision of alternatives for the prayers, including an alternative Canon and a choice of two Post-Communions.

From 1525 Bucer's influence gradually increased until he became the ecclesiastical leader at Strasbourg. His theological position was a *via media* between Lutheranism and Zwinglianism, and his influence upon public worship was towards simplification and the laying of greater emphasis on the didactic element, so we have the introduction of the sermon. Six new revisions were published in 1525, and a further seven between 1526 and 1539. As this is as far as it is necessary for our purpose to trace the development of the Strasbourg rites, the structural outline of Bucer's *Psalter*, 1539, may be given:

LITURGY OF THE WORD

Confession of Sins (choice of three)
Scriptural words of pardon: 1 Tim. 1: 15
Absolution
Psalm or Hymn

[1] W. D. Maxwell, *John Knox's Genevan Service Book, 1556*, 1931, p. 26 (hereafter referred to as *JKGSB*).

Kyrie eleison (sometimes omitted)
Gloria in excelsis (sometimes omitted)
Collect for Illumination
Metrical psalm (meanwhile minister goes to pulpit)
Gospel (read in course)
Sermon (based on Gospel)

LITURGY OF THE FAITHFUL

Exhortation on right reception
Apostles' Creed (preparation of elements)
Salutation
Prayer of Consecration (choice of three)
    Intercessions
    Consecration
Lord's Prayer
Exhortation (omitted if one after sermon used)
Scriptural Warrant
Fraction
Delivery
Communion (meanwhile *Gott sey gelobet*, or other psalm, sung)
Post-Communion (choice of four)
Aaronic Blessing
Dismissal

Attention may be drawn here to the fact that in the Anaphora the intercessions come first as in the Roman Canon, and not at the end as in the later Eastern rites.

In Strasbourg, in the German Church, weekly communion was the rule, but by 1538 a practice, which concerns us so far as the norm of the Morning Service for the Lord's Day of the Reformed rite is concerned, was becoming common. Weekly celebration had been the practice in the Cathedral and in the parish churches, but now in the latter there was only a monthly celebration. The reason for this is not easy to determine. It may have been owing to the influence of Zurich, which will be discussed later, or the result of the stern warning against unworthy communicating inserted into the rite by Bucer,[1] or because infrequent communicating was the custom in the mediaeval church.

---

[1] L. Büchsenschütz, *Histoire des liturgies en langue allemande dans l'Église de Strasbourg au seizième siècle*, 1900, p. 106.

Whatever the reason, it is important, as Dr. Hageman says,

> to notice the provision made by Bucer, and later by Calvin, for those Sundays when there was no celebration of the Eucharist. We do not find, as with Zwingli[1] or Farel,[2] two separate services, one for preaching and the other for the Eucharist. There is but one service for the Lord's Day, rubricated to show at what point and in what manner it may be terminated whenever the Eucharist is not to be celebrated . . . The Eucharist is seen as a necessary part of the cultic act, so necessary that it must determine the structure of the service even when it is not celebrated.[3]

This meant that the Sunday Morning Service, when the Lord's Supper was not celebrated, omitted all that pertained to Communion. The rest of the service was retained. It was a parallel to the *Missa Catechumenorum* of the early church, although it must be remembered that there it never stood alone, but after the dismissal of the catechumens regularly reached its climax and fulfilment in the *Missa fidelium*.

Such a statement as that of Dr. Brilioth, that for Bucer and Calvin "the sacrament was treated as an appendage to the preaching-service",[4] is completely inaccurate. Rather we should say the Sunday Morning Service is an abbreviated Lord's Supper, the Eucharist being the norm.

The following is the structural outline of the Sunday Morning Service at Strasbourg when Communion was not celebrated:

Scripture Sentence: "Our help is in the name. . . ."
Confession of sins
Scripture sentence of remission
Absolution
Psalm or Hymn
Kyrie eleison (sometimes omitted)
Gloria in excelsis (sometimes omitted)
Collect for Illumination
Psalm (meanwhile minister goes to pulpit)
Gospel (read in course)
Sermon (based on Gospel)
Apostles' Creed
Intercessions (choice of three)
Lord's Prayer
Psalm
Aaronic Blessing   Dismissal

[1] H. Zwingli, *Epicheiresis.*   [2] G. Farel, *La Manière et Fasson.*
[3] H. G. Hageman, *Pulpit and Table*, 1962, p. 26.
[4] Y. Brilioth, *op. cit.*, pp. 173–4.

In the year 1538, because of his sacramental views, Calvin was expelled from Geneva and became minister to the congregation of French exiles at Strasbourg, and these were the services which Calvin found in use when he came to Strasbourg. They were an important determining factor in his liturgical reforms.

Until then, the German authorities had not permitted the French congregation to celebrate the Lord's Supper, but, shortly after his arrival, as a "special privilege", permission was granted for a monthly celebration in accordance with the custom in the German churches under the leadership of Bucer. This made the compilation of a Service-Book necessary. It is not known whether or not there was some agreement, for, if so, it has not been recorded, that the services of the French congregation should approximate to those of the German churches; in any event, as Dr. W. D. Maxwell says, "Calvin seems to have had a high opinion of the worship established in Strasbourg, for he adopted it almost word for word."[1] "As for the Sunday Prayers", says Calvin; "I took the form of Strasbourg, and borrowed the greater part of it."[2] This work, entitled *La Manyère de faire prières aux églises françoyses*, was completed about the end of 1539 or the spring of 1540. A reprint was issued in 1542 under the direction of Pierre Brully. On his return to Geneva in 1541, Calvin introduced these services there. Before discussing the Genevan rites, we must refer to the later editions of the Strasbourg rite.

In 1545 Calvin prepared a third edition with the title *La Forme des Prières* for the use of his former congregation in Strasbourg,[3] in the preface of which he leaves us in no doubt as to his views concerning the ideal Sunday Morning Service. He writes:

We begin with the confession of our sins, adding readings from the Law and the Gospel (that is, sentences of remission) . . . and after we are assured that as Jesus Christ has righteousness and life in Himself, and that He lives for the sake of the Father, so we are justified in Jesus Christ and live in a new life by the same Jesus Christ . . . we continue with psalms, hymns of praise, the reading of the Gospel . . . and . . . quickened and stirred by the reading and preaching of the Gospel, and the confession of our faith (that is, Apostles' Creed) . . . it follows that we must pray for the salvation of all men for the life of Christ should be greatly enkindled within us. Now the life of Christ

[1] W. D. Maxwell, *An Outline of Christian Worship*, 1936, p. 112.
[2] *Corpus Reformatorum*, ix, 894 (hereafter referred to as *CR*).
[3] *CR*, v, 193-7.

consists in this, namely, to seek and to save that which is lost. Fittingly, then, we pray for all estates of men. And because we receive Jesus Christ truly in this Sacrament . . . we worship Him in spirit and in truth; and receive the Eucharist with reverence, concluding the whole mystery with praise and thanksgiving. This, then, is the whole order and reason for its administration in this manner; and it agrees also with its administration in the ancient Church of the apostles, of the martyrs, and of the holy fathers.[1]

The *Liturgia sacra* of Pullain, who had been a successor of Calvin in Strasbourg, is really a fourth edition. He had sought refuge with his congregation of Walloons in England, where this work was first published in 1551. It is really a Latin translation of Calvin's Strasbourg *La Forme* with the rubrics expanded so that English scholars might know the forms of worship in his congregation. A second edition of this rite was published in Frankfurt in 1554. It is only a simplification of the London edition, but is important for us because it was consulted by John Knox and his committee at Frankfurt when compiling the *Forme of Prayers*, 1556.

To show the relationship of Calvin's Strasbourg rite to that of the German, the structural outline for the Lord's Supper may be set out as follows:

LITURGY OF THE WORD
Scripture sentence (same as in German rite)
Confession of sins (same as second alternative in German rite)
Sentences of remission (same as in German rite)
Absolution
Metrical Decalogue: First Table (same as Bucer's practice)
Prayer for instruction in God's law (same as Bucer)
Metrical Decalogue: Second Table (same as Bucer)
Collect for Illumination
Scripture Lesson
Sermon

LITURGY OF THE FAITHFUL
Intercessions (same as third alternative in German rite)
Lord's Prayer (in a long paraphrase)
Apostles' Creed, and preparation of elements
Consecration Prayer (based on third alternative in German rite)
Lord's Prayer
Words of Institution: Scriptural Warrant (same as in German rite)

[1] *CR*, v, 194–6.

Exhortation
Fraction
Delivery
Communion (Psalms sung meanwhile)
Post-Communion (same as second alternative in German rite)
Nunc dimittis (in metre)
Aaronic Blessing (as in German rite)

Concerning this rite, Dr. W. D. Maxwell states, "Calvin . . , for a reason unknown, placed the Creed after the Great Prayer, but there is support for this in some of the primitive liturgies."[1] By "primitive liturgies" Maxwell presumably meant the later Eastern rites of St. James, St. Basil, and St. Chrysostom, as the Creed was not used in the early liturgies until the fifth century. In these rites the Liturgy of the Faithful begins with the prayers of the faithful, whereas in the Roman Mass the priest says *Oremus*, but no prayer follows. In view of this, the writer feels that Maxwell misses the real constructive significance of Calvin's order, and instead of wording it as he has done would prefer to say that Calvin took the intercessions out of the prayer of consecration and restored the prayers of the faithful, which had dropped out of the Roman Mass.

Calvin was recalled to Geneva in 1541 and the rite used there by him was first published in 1542 with the title *La Forme des Prières*. This was a simplified form of the rite which he had used in Strasbourg, but the structure and subject-matter were the same. Their relationship may be seen from the following outline:

LITURGY OF THE WORD

Scripture sentence (same as in Strasbourg)
Confession of sins (same as in Strasbourg)
Metrical psalm
Collect for Illumination
Scripture Lesson
Sermon

LITURGY OF THE FAITHFUL

Intercessions (same as in Strasbourg)
Lord's Prayer (in a long paraphrase; same as in Strasbourg)
Apostles' Creed, and preparation of elements

[1] *JKGSB*, p. 32.

Scriptural Warrant (same as in Strasbourg)
Exhortation
Prayer of Consecration (same as in Strasbourg)
Fraction
Delivery
Communion (psalm sung, or Scripture read, meanwhile)
Post-communion (same as in Strasbourg)
Aaronic Blessing (same as in Strasbourg)

When one compares this outline with that of the French rite at Strasbourg, one notices at once that the Genevan rite is much more meagre; but, as this is probably the result of civil interference, the Strasbourg rite may be taken as a better indication of the preferences of Calvin. In Geneva, because of the opposition of the civil authorities, weekly communion was not possible. Here, also, the Sunday Morning Service took the form of an Ante-Communion. Commenting on the Sacrament of the Lord's Supper being placed in a separate section in Calvin's *La Forme*, Lacharet writes, "Be that as it may, in Calvin's conception, Christian worship includes two separate parts: the ordinary service was only the first part of it; a service with Holy Communion . . . ought to complete it and to give to it its natural conclusion and true consummation."[1]

Calvin, all his life, endeavoured to establish a weekly celebration of the Lord's Supper, but he was never able to do so. In the *Institutes*, written before he came to Geneva, he states, "The Lord's Supper should be celebrated in the Christian congregation once a week at the very least."[2] In 1561 he left on record his disappointment with Genevan practice, "I have taken care to record publicly that our custom is defective, so that those who come after me may be able to correct it the more freely and easily."[3]

The Genevan *La Forme*, 1542, was translated into Latin with the title *Formula sacramentorum* and published by John Crispin later in the same year. This was consulted by Knox and his associates when compiling the *Forme of Prayers*, 1556. All later editions of the Genevan *La Forme* follow that of 1542 closely; and the 1547 edition, or possibly that of 1549, but more probably the former, was translated into English by Huycke in 1550. This, too, was consulted by Knox and his colleagues.

---

[1] *Revue Chrétienne*, 1886, p. 772.
[2] *CR*, x, 1, 7.
[3] *CR*, x, 1,213; iv, 1051–2.

Many have criticized the Genevan rite for its bareness, and have described it as cold and meagre. This, however, is a modern inference, for in the sixteenth century such an opinion was eliminated by two factors: firstly, the introduction of the vernacular so that the people were able to understand the service; and, secondly, the introduction of congregational singing. About a year after coming to Strasbourg, Calvin made a collection of some of Marot's metrical psalms and some paraphrases, and published them under the title *Aulcuns Pseaumes et Cantiques mys en chant*; and, although Farel had outlawed singing in Geneva, Calvin saw its great possibilities and importance and reintroduced it, actively encouraging musicians, such as Franc, Davantes, Bourgeois, Goudimel and Marot.

Before turning to the Reformed rites in English, a word must be said about the liturgical reforms of Zwingli in Zurich. It is not necessary to go into detail. To Zwingli there is only one means of grace, namely, the preaching of the Word. To him, the Eucharist is really another form of preaching, the dramatic re-enactment of what on other occasions has been proclaimed in the sermon. The Lord's Supper is a meal of remembrance in which the communicant confesses that Jesus has died for his sins and renews his obligation to Christian fellowship. Because of this, Zwingli did not hold to a weekly celebration, but a quarterly, at Christmas, Easter, Pentecost, and the Festival of St. Felix and St. Regula, the patron saints of Zurich (September 11). At all other times, the service was a preaching service which Zwingli based on Ulrich Surgant's 1506 revision of the Prone. "The divorce of Word and Sacrament," writes Dr. Hageman, "the transformation of the Sunday service into a sermon, the quarterly celebration of the Supper—these were Zwingli's deliberate design, a cultus that derived directly from his creed."[1] While this, in the opinion of the writer, is less than fair to Zwingli,[2] yet it has to be admitted that this understanding of his teaching has left a lasting mark on the worship and practice of all the Reformed churches.

---

[1] H. G. Hageman, *op. cit.*, p. 21.

[2] N. Micklem (ed.), *Christian Worship*, 1936, pp. 137-53. A. Barclay, *The Protestant Doctrine of the Lord's Supper*, 1927.

III

THE REFORMED RITE IN ENGLISH

MARY'S SUCCESSION to the throne of England in 1553 was followed by a period of persecution so that many who had supported the movement for reform had to fly to the Continent, where they found refuge in cities such as Strasbourg, Emden, Zurich, Frankfurt and Geneva. Our interest centres upon the last two. Pullain with his congregation had already settled in Frankfurt and had been granted the right to worship in the Weissfrauenkirche. He welcomed the English exiles and advised them to petition the city council for permission to reside there. On July 14, the Council

> granted that they should have liberty to preach and minister the sacraments, in that Church which the French men had, the French one day and the English another day and upon Sunday to choose also the hours as they could agree among themselves, but it was with this commandment, that the English should not dissent from the French men in doctrine, or ceremonies, lest they should thereby minister occasion of offence, and willed farther, that before they entered their Church, they should approve and subscribe the same confession of faith, that the French men had then presented.[1]

These conditions were accepted unanimously, but difficulties arose as to their exact meaning, and caused a division among the members of the congregation so far as the form of worship was concerned. Among other attempts made to reach a settlement, in January, 1555, Knox, Whittingham, Gilby, Fox and Cole were appointed a committee to draw up a Service-Book. "Whatever", writes Dr. W. D. Maxwell, "is to be said concerning the merits or demerits of this service book, it could never be reasonably described as a fair compromise between Anglicanism and Calvinism."[2] Consequently it was rejected by the congregation, and the "Liturgy of Compromise" was drawn up. The contention, however, after a few weeks grew more vexed than before, and eventually Knox had to flee from Frankfurt. Thence he came to

---

[1] *Brief Discourse of the Troubles at Frankfort*, 1846, p. vi; P. Hume Brown, *John Knox*, 1895, ii, 299.

[2] *JKGSB*, p. 6.

Geneva, where he was welcomed by Calvin, and the City Council assured him of their hospitality and their desire to give refuge, Calvin himself presenting the case of the English-speaking Calvinists who had arrived in the city to the Council for its sympathetic consideration. The work of organization proceeded, although Knox was in Scotland, Goodman and Gilby being elected ministers. Knox returned, as minister, in 1556. One of the first tasks to be undertaken was to prepare an Order for Public Worship, which task was completed before Knox's return. The form drawn up at Frankfurt, before the "Liturgy of Compromise", was now revived and perhaps, but this is not certain, slightly revised. However, there was no substantial alteration; but a preface, fifty metrical psalms in English, and an English translation of Calvin's *Catechism* were added. This was issued from the press of John Crispin on February 10, 1556; and remained, until the dissolution of the congregation with the accession of Elizabeth to the English throne, the standard of worship. Communion was celebrated monthly in harmony with Genevan practice. The following structural outline shows the relationship of the *Forme of Prayers*, 1556, to Calvin's *La Forme*:

LITURGY OF THE WORD

Confession of sins (choice of two, one based on Calvin)
Prayer for pardon
Metrical Psalm
Prayer for Illumination
Scripture reading
Sermon

LITURGY OF THE FAITHFUL

Intercessions (reminiscent of Calvin, but an independent compilation)
Lord's Prayer
Apostles' Creed (read by Minister because no metrical version)
Psalm; elements prepared
Scriptural Warrant (as in Calvin)
Exhortation
Prayer of Consecration (reminiscent of Calvin, but independent compilation)
Fraction
Delivery

Communion (Scripture read meanwhile)
Post-communion (based on Calvin)
Metrical psalm ciii
Aaronic or Apostolic Blessing

In spite of slight deviations from Calvin, it remains perfectly clear that Calvin's Genevan *La Forme* was the governing influence and main source of the English Genevan Service-Book, although evidence of an independent spirit is not lacking, for new intercessions and a new prayer of consecration appear, both of which are similar to Calvin's in spirit and doctrinal content.

This book exiles returning to England and Scotland brought with them, but it was not until the return of John Knox in 1559 that the use of the book became general in Scotland.

Before 1560 many in Scotland had used the *Book of Common Prayer*, 1552,[1] and in 1557 it was adopted by the "Lords of the Congregation".[2] While this decision had not the force of law, it had the consent of all the Reformed party. However, in 1560, the first *Book of Discipline* states, "The Order of Geneva, which now is used in some of our kirks, is sufficient to instruct the diligent reader how both these sacraments may be rightly ministered,"[3] from which one may infer that, although the first *Book of Discipline* never became law, yet, because of the tremendous influence it exercised, the sacraments were administered according to the Genevan Order. The first General Assembly of the Church of Scotland, in 1560, directed that "the sacraments be ministered after the Order of the Kirk of Geneva".[4] This was confirmed by the fourth General Assembly in 1562, and in 1564 an edition was published bearing on its title page "Approved and received by the Church of Scotland".

The Book in its Scottish form followed Calvin's *La Forme* even more closely than the Genevan Service-Book had done. Thus, the confession of sins which Calvin had adopted from pre-Reformation sources was given primary place instead of the longer confession of the *Forme of Prayers*, 1556. Again, the prayer of consecration in the Genevan Book had been a loose paraphrase rather than a translation of the similar prayer in Calvin. This was retained, but a translation of Calvin's prayer was added as an alternative. As well as this, some of the passages

[1] W. McMillan, *The Worship of the Scottish Reformed Church*, 1931, p. 35.
[2] J. Knox, *Works*, ed. D. Laing, 1855, i, 275.
[3] *First Book of Discipline*, 2.
[4] J. Knox, *op. cit.*, ii, 186.

where the Genevan book had followed the *Book of Common Prayer*, 1552, were replaced by the corresponding sections in Calvin's liturgy. During 1562-4, there was considerable revision and expansion: new prayers drawn from Continental and Scottish sources were added and the metrical psalter was completed. Thus the *Book of Common Order*, 1564, was brought closer to the form of prayers which Calvin had received in Strasbourg, and which was an evangelical rendering of the ancient service of the Church.

In England, from Elizabethan times, there was a sharp division between the parties later known as "Anglicans" and "Puritans". We must distinguish here between "Liturgy" and "Ceremony". The former is what the Christian community says, whether in speech or song, whether through itself or through its ministry, in its acts of worship. The latter is the way in which it is said, the gestures, actions, settings, which accompany it. The Puritans, while differing from the Anglicans over "Ceremony", were just as liturgical as they were, although they preferred the Genevan Order to the *Book of Common Prayer*, but the division gave rise to a group of extremists within the Puritan party, who completely rejected the use of Service-Books and Liturgies. The extremists or Brownists were principally opposed to (i) read prayers, (ii) the use of the *Gloria Patri*, (iii) the use of the Creed, (iv) the use of the Lord's Prayer, and (v) kneeling for prayer on entering the pulpit.

At the same time as the Brownist controversy was in progress, other attempts were being made to alter the worship of the Church of Scotland. To understand these, it is necessary to bear in mind the constitution of the Church during the reign of James I. Put briefly, it was as follows: the king supported the titular bishops, and by his own authority interfered with the affairs of the Church, usually through the bishops; yet the presbyteries and the General Assembly still existed, and the king endeavoured to get his will carried out by Acts of Assembly. Thus it will be seen that the Church was both diocesan and presbyterial, since it had bishops and also presbyteries. There were in the Church two parties, those who leaned to the presbyterian side and those who leaned towards a diocesan episcopacy. It must be remembered, however, that the bishops were not extreme diocesans of the Laudian type, and that the majority were well content with the dual organization. The real cause of such trouble as arose was not the bishops but royal interference.

The first suggestions for revision of worship came from within the Church itself. At the Assembly of 1601 it was proposed, (i) that the translation of the Bible should be revised, (ii) that there should be a revision of the metrical psalter, and (iii) that the *Book of Common Order* should be made "more convenient for the times".[1] Nothing was done along any of these lines, but with regard to the third it was decided that nothing in it should be altered, but that if anyone wished to suggest additional prayers these might be considered and sanctioned by a future Assembly.[2]

In 1614 and 1615 the king, by proclamation, tried to enforce the celebration of Communion at Easter. This raised little trouble, because "Easter had in some parishes kept its ground as one of the seasons of the Communion", though a few ministers disobeyed the proclamation.[3] Next the king sent instructions to the Assembly of 1616 that they were to prepare a new form of service "which shall be read in every church in common prayer and before preaching every Sabbath by the Reader where there is one, and where there is not by the Minister before he conceive his own prayer, that the common people may learn it, and by custom serve God rightly".[4]

The reference to the Reader makes it necessary to say a word of explanation about the Reader's service. In the 1586, 1587, 1602, and other editions, of the *Forme of Prayers*, 1556, used by the Puritans in England, we find the first rubric of the Sunday Morning Service enlarged to: "Upon the days appointed for the preaching of the Word, when a convenient number of the congregation are come together, that they make fruit of their presence till the assembly be full, one appointed by the eldership, shall read some chapters of the canonical books of scripture, singing psalms between at his direction, and this reading to be in order as the books and chapters follow, that so from time to time the Holy Scriptures may be read throughout. . . ."[5] So arose the custom of prefixing the Reader's Service to the Sunday Morning Service. In Scotland a similar practice soon obtained and we find Readers appointed from 1560 onwards.[6]

In obedience to the king's injunction, the Assembly appointed Patrick Galloway, Peter Hewat, John Adamson and William Erskine, all of whom belonged to the Presbyterian party, to revise the *Book of*

---

[1] A. Peterkin (ed.), *Booke of the Universall Kirk of Scotland*, 1839, iii, 970.
[2] *Ibid.*, iii, 970–1.
[3] G. W. Sprott, *Scottish Liturgies of James VI*, 1901, p. xvi.
[4] *Ibid.*, p. xix.
[5] P. Hall, *Reliquiae liturgicae*, 1847, i, 17.
[6] J. Knox, *op. cit.*, ii, 195–6, 238.

Common Order with this end in view, but the labours of this committee never received official sanction.

Meanwhile, the king tried to deprive the Assembly of its powers, and to take upon himself the supreme legislative power for the church. The bishops were pressed to prepare a new Prayer Book, and the matter was left in the hands of William Cowper, bishop of Galloway, but nothing came of his proposals. These two efforts at revision are of interest, however, in that as Hewat's form shows us the presbyterian ideals of the time, so Cowper's shows us the episcopalian.

In 1618 the king pressed more strongly for the alterations in worship which he desired. The Assembly met in Perth in August of that year. To this the king sent "Five Articles" and demanded that they should be passed. They were strongly opposed, but the opposition was cut short, for the question was put in the form, "whether they would obey the king or not". The royal commissioner, also, told the members of Assembly that they would not be allowed to depart until they satisfied the king's desire. So the Articles were passed, though many ministers voted against them.

These Articles required (i) kneeling to receive Communion, (ii) the private celebration of the Communion for the sick, (iii) private baptism, (iv) confirmation, and (v) the observance of Christmas, Good Friday, Easter, and Whitsun Day.[1] With regard to the first, the presbyterian practice had been for the minister and people to kneel for the prayer of consecration and take their seats at the Table before the elements were distributed. There was also the question of "adoration" dealt with in the famous Black rubric. The objection to the second and third was the same, namely, an objection to administering the sacraments anywhere except in the presence of the congregation. Calvin had desired that the sick, and especially the dying, should receive the sacrament of the Lord's Supper.[2] His view was that the sacrament should be celebrated at the sick person's bedside. Beza, Calvin's successor in Geneva, on the other hand, directed that this should be done by carrying the elements to the sick from the church immediately after the administration there. There is some evidence to show that this latter had been the practice in many places in Scotland before 1618, and in all the disputing about the second article no one suggested that any objection would be taken to this method of communicating the sick.[3]

[1] A. Peterkin, *op. cit.*, pp. 1165–6.
[2] *CR*, x, 213; xvii, 311–12.
[3] W. McMillan, *op. cit.*, p. 211.

The presbyterian objection to Confirmation by a diocesan bishop is obvious, for the Aberdeen Assembly, two years earlier, had held that "the parochial bishop could confirm as well as the diocesan".[1] Today the objection to observing Christmas and other festivals seems strange. The banning of these festivals was due, at first, to a desire to stamp out the superstitions associated with them, and also to curb the profane revelry which marked them. Calvin, in Geneva, observed the feasts of Christ's birth, death, resurrection and ascension, as well as Pentecost. In Scotland, the only one banned by the first *Book of Discipline* was Christmas, and it was banned as a "feast of our Lady", not as the festival of Christ's birth.[2] The compilers were well acquainted with the distinction between a minor saint's day and a greater Christian festival. It was an abandonment in theory rather than in practice, for in many parishes the chief festivals continued to be observed.[3] The objection to the fifth article was based on the fact that their observance is not commanded in scripture, and it is, therefore, held to be an offence against Christian liberty to enforce them.

The royal fiat was resented as an intrusion, and, needless to say, the five articles were strenuously resisted in some quarters. Confusion and riots followed the efforts of the king to enforce kneeling communion.[4] Private baptism and communion were seldom, if ever, used; and the diocesan bishops never attempted to hold confirmations.[5] The festivals, even in some places where previously they had been observed, were ignored, except by those who wished to stand well at court. However, the fact that one of the chief complaints of the minority at Perth was that they were not allowed to vote on the articles one by one shows that some of them would have found more favour than others.[6] Indeed, the Assemblies of the preceding years at Aberdeen and St. Andrews had virtually allowed articles two to five.[7]

The accession of Charles I to the throne brought no relief to the Church of Scotland so far as royal and state dictation in matters spiritual and ecclesiastical was concerned. Early in his reign he let it be known that he intended to carry out and enforce the ordinances and

---

[1] T. Leishman, *Ritual of the Church of Scotland*, 1890, p. 368.
[2] *First Book of Discipline*, I.
[3] W. McMillan, *op. cit.*, pp. 299–329.
[4] *Ibid.*, pp. 178–89.
[5] *Ibid.*, p. 231.
[6] T. Leishman, *op. cit.*, p. 367.
[7] A. Peterkin, *op. cit.*, pp. 589–99; T. Leishman, *op. cit.*, p. 367.

injunctions of his father. In 1636 was issued the *Canons and Constitutions Ecclesiastical; gathered and put in form for the government of the Church of Scotland. Ratified and Approved by His Majesty's Royal Warrant, and ordained to be observed by the Clergy, and all others whom they concern*; and, in 1637, the *Book of Common Prayer and Administration of the Sacraments, and other parts of divine service for the use of the Church of Scotland*, commonly known as "Laud's Liturgy". It is unnecessary here to go into details of how Charles attempted to force this Service-Book upon the Church of Scotland, for the story of the riot in St. Giles' is well known.

It is a misnomer to call it "Laud's Liturgy", because it was compiled by two Scottish bishops, Wedderburn of Dunblane and Maxwell of Ross. It is not necessary to examine the rite in detail; suffice it to say that it was a noble liturgy and really deserved a better fate. At the same time two very common misunderstandings about the "Liturgy of 1637" ought to be removed. The first concerns the presbyterian objection to it. It is frequently said that this was an objection to the reading of prayers from a book. Such was not the case. The congregation in St. Giles' were perfectly accustomed to read prayers, and immediately before the riot had heard the Reader reading the old prayers for the last time. Presbyteries and parishes, and towns and individuals sent in great numbers of petitions against the new liturgy, but not one of these mentions the reading of prayers as an objection to it. The real objection was twofold: first, because it was alien to the custom and use of the Church of Scotland, and second, because the prayers in it were invariable, whereas the *Book of Common Order* provided optional variants for all prayers, and allowed the prayers themselves to be altered.

The second misunderstanding is one which is common among Anglicans, and is sometimes taken up and repeated by Presbyterians. The Anglican scholar compares the "Liturgy of 1637" with the English Prayer Book of the time, from his point of view, and considers it much "higher". He then remarks on the stupidity of Charles and Laud in trying to force upon the Church of Scotland, not merely the *Book of Common Prayer*, 1552, but actually a more high church version of it. Such an outlook does a grave injustice to Laud. The *Book of Common Prayer*, 1549, was altered in 1552. Some of the alterations may have been in a Puritan direction, but others were towards Zwinglianism,[1] and so were as offensive to a Calvinist as to a Romanist. It may be

[1] G. Dix, *op. cit.*, pp. 656, 659, 668.

safely said that there is not one difference between the *Book of Common Prayer*, 1552, and the "Liturgy of 1637" which would make the latter more objectionable to Presbyterians than the former. To take just one example, an issue which arose again at the Savoy Conference,[1] the "Liturgy of 1637" in the Communion Service restored the epiclesis, which had been in the *Book of Common Prayer*, 1549, but was omitted in that of 1552, and also the form of words to be used by the Minister as he delivered the elements to the communicants.[2] This change may seem to the Anglican to make the "Liturgy of 1637" more "high church", but it actually made it more Calvinistic and brought it nearer to the practice of the Church of Scotland.[3] No doubt these changes were such as to please Laud, the high churchman, but they were also such as to please Calvinistic Scotland and later the Westminster divines.[4]

The real reason for the rejection of the "Liturgy of 1637" was the attempt of the king to enforce its use by an Order in Council without consulting the Scottish Church. That one of the main objects of the rite was to improve the worship of the church cannot, and should not, be denied, but the result was disastrous, for it was not till well into the second half of the nineteenth century that the ground then lost began to be recovered.[5]

The early Scottish Reformed tradition was first broken by the Westminster *Directory for the Public Worship of God*, 1645, part of the Puritan attempt to provide a basis of uniformity for the churches in Scotland, England and Ireland. The Assembly of Divines at Westminster, it should be remembered, was an assembly of clergy of the Church of England, to which the Scottish Church sent commissioners, who could take part in the deliberations, but not vote; and each member took the vow,

> I . . . , do seriously promise and vow, in the presence of Almighty God, that in this Assembly, whereof I am a member, I will maintain nothing in point of doctrine, but what I believe to be most agreeable to the word of God; nor

[1] G. F. Nuttall and O. Chadwick, *From Uniformity to Unity, 1662–1962*, 1962, pp. 89–149.

[2] F. E. Brightman, *The English Rite*, 1921, ii, 692, 701; J. Cooper, *Liturgy of 1637 (Laud's Liturgy)*, 1904, pp. 129, 131.

[3] J. Row, *Historie of the Kirk of Scotland*, ed. T. Thompson, 1842, p. 338; D. Calderwood, *Altare Damascenum*, 1623, pp. 777–8.

[4] T. Leishman, *The Westminster Directory*, 1868, pp. 310–11.

[5] J. Cooper, *op. cit.*, pp. xi–xii.

in point of discipline, but what may make most for God's glory, and the peace and good of this Church.[1]

The members of the Westminster Assembly were divided among themselves, with the result that the *Directory* was, as Dr. H. Davies says, "a compromise between the three parties, the English Presbyterians, the Scottish Presbyterians and the Independents".[2] In view of this it is not surprising to find that on many points the *Directory* says nothing, or gives only a general direction. In this connection it must be pointed out that the text of the *Directory* must never be taken as representing Scottish practice, because many of the points in dispute are covered in the two adopting Acts of the Scottish Assembly. The *Directory* favoured the practices of the Independents, and during the Commonwealth the General Assembly was silenced. "The Church, deprived of its supreme court," says Leishman, "lost all unity and continuity of action, and soon the anarchy of the civil estate was reflected by the ecclesiastical."[3]

While the text of the *Directory*, studied alongside the Act of Assembly on February 7, 1645, shows that the eucharistic norm was retained, yet the belief, incorrect though it was, that the revolt of 1637 was against the use of a liturgy, the growing influence of the ideas of the Independents, and the fact that upon the recall of the Stuarts there was no attempt to introduce either the "Liturgy of 1637" or the *Book of Common Prayer*, 1552, or to restore the *Book of Common Order*, 1564, led to a chaotic situation in which, broadly speaking, "every man did that which was right in his own eyes". This was followed by two centuries of decadence, and it was not until the second half of the nineteenth century that a revival of interest in worship took place. The principal thing to notice here is that after 1645 the Service-Book became a directory for ministers, and was no longer a book in the hands of the people. Up to this, the Reformed Churches "were no less liturgical than the Lutheran or Anglican Churches; they came into the world with fully-defined and completely expressed orders of worship".[4] This was now completely changed.

The chief changes in the worship of the Church of Scotland, during the latter half of the seventeenth century were: (a) the celebration of

---

[1] A. F. Mitchell and J. Struthers, *Minutes of the Westminster Assembly, 1644–1649*, 1874, p. lxxx.

[2] H. Davies, *The Worship of the English Puritans*, 1948, p. 157.

[3] T. Leishman, *The Ritual of the Church of Scotland*, 1890, p. 389.

[4] H. G. Hageman, *op. cit.*, p. 14.

Communion became very infrequent, although the *Directory* had said, "The Communion, or supper of the Lord, is frequently to be celebrated"; (b) because of the Protester or Remonstrant schism "multiple services" became the custom, which a pamphlet of 1657 describes as follows:

> Our dissenting brethren have taken up a new and irregular way . . . They do not now usually celebrate that ordinance but they have a great many ministers gathered unto it, six and seven, and sometimes double and more, whose congregations most part are left destitute of preaching that day; great confluences from all the country, and many congregations about, are gathered at them; and on every day of their meeting, which are Saturday, the Lord's Day, and Monday, many of these ministers do preach successively one after another; so that three or four, and sometimes more, do preach at their preparation, and as many on the Monday following. And on the Lord's Day sometimes three or four preach before they go to the Action, besides those who preach to the multitude of people that cannot be contained in the Church.[1]

(c) There was a change in the style of preaching, of which Baillie says, it "runs out in a discourse on some common head, in a high, romancing, unscriptural style, tickling the ear for the present, and moving the affections in some, but leaving . . . little or nought to the memory and understanding",[2] and Wodrow describes as "skimming the text";[3] and (d) the posture for prayer changed to sitting in many places.[4]

The eighteenth century produced no great change, the only innovation being the introduction of the practice of the reading of sermons. Sitting for prayer, which began in the seventeenth century, was becoming more common. The paraphrases were added to the Psalter. In all essentials public worship remained "Brownist", and the mode of celebrating the sacrament of the Lord's Supper introduced by the Protesters continued. This state of affairs continued right up to the middle of the nineteenth century. Dr. Story says:

> The public services of the Church of Scotland had become probably the baldest and rudest in Christendom. The parish kirks, owing to the niggardliness of the heritors, were comfortless and coarsely furnished. The music was rough and untrained; only in a few of the town churches was it rendered with any attempt at taste or skill. The Bible was scarcely read. The prayers

---

[1] T. Leishman, *op. cit.*, pp. 390–1.
[2] R. Baillie, *Letters and Journals*, ed. D. Laing, 1841, iii, 258.
[3] R. Wodrow, *Analecta*, 1842, i, 168.
[4] T. Leishman, *op. cit.*, p. 395.

were reduced in number to two at the most, and were drearily long and uninteresting. The Lord's Prayer (and Creed) were never heard. The sermon was the great feature of the service; and it was too often a "screed of dull doctrine or of cold morality".[1]

As late as 1905, Dr. G. W. Sprott writes:

Till within the memory of many still living the order of Public Worship was —Praise (four verses of a psalm), Prayer, (Praise), Lecture or Sermon, Prayer, Psalm or Paraphrase, Benediction. . . . The mutilated form of the Protesters had come to be regarded as embodying that purity of worship which the Reformers restored, and for which the Covenanters had fought and died. The defence of old Reformed usages, such as the reading of Scripture and of prayers, the reciting of the Creed and the Lord's Prayer, and the singing of the Gloria, by the Covenanting Assemblies and their leaders, Henderson, Douglas, Ramsey, Calderwood, and Baillie, against "sectarian conceits" borrowed from England, was entirely forgotten. The educated opinion of the country was at one with the belief of the common people.[2]

The revival came in the second half of the nineteenth century, and for a period the central figure was Dr. Robert Lee, minister of Old Greyfriars Church, Edinburgh. The movement, however, was principally fostered by the strong body of scholars who formed the Church Service Society, which was founded on January 31, 1865. Two years later this Society issued a Service-Book, *Euchologion*, which, in its various editions, brought great enrichment to the public worship of the Church of Scotland. While the Church Service Society is a "private one",[3] something must be said of its work, because to it the revival of worship in Scotland, and in English-speaking presbyterianism, is much indebted.

In the revival a serious liturgical change was made, in spite of the protests of the best liturgical scholars in the Church Service Society, which continues to the present day. In the first five editions of the *Euchologion* the eucharistic norm was followed, but in the sixth a change was introduced. Dr. W. D. Maxwell writes:

The importance of Anglican Morning and Evening Prayer lies in the influence that its structure, and in part its content, has had upon the worship

---

[1] R. H. Story, *Reformed Ritual in Scotland*, 1890, p. 36. Words in brackets added by writer.

[2] G. W. Sprott, *The Book of Common Order* (*Euchologion*, seventh edition), 1905, pp. vii–viii.

[3] Constitution, 6.

of the Reformed Churches, particularly in English speaking countries, during the last half century or more. What was designed and intended for services of daily prayer, a beautiful but subsidiary order, has been adopted, with certain alterations, as the norm of the weekly worship in many of the non-Anglican Churches. This development, at a time when the standard of worship had declined, brought with it many new enrichments; but worship that takes its structure from Morning Prayer must inevitably lack the centrality and objectiveness which characterize the Eucharist or even Ante-Communion.[1]

Dr. Thomas Leishman had, in his 1868 edition of the *Westminster Directory*, shown that the rubric at the close of the section "On Prayer before Sermon" was added because of the practice of the Scottish Church. Although this knowledge was available, when the structure of Morning Prayer was studied it was found to approximate to that of the Scottish services if the old Reader's service was restored. Structurally, the chief difference was that in the Scottish service the intercessions and thanksgiving followed the sermon. Also, an examination of the text of the *Directory* showed that it was not unrelated structurally to Morning Prayer. Once this agreement had become established in the minds of the reformers, it was natural that they should turn to Morning Prayer as the norm of Sunday worship. There was a failure to grasp that the "rationale" of the two services differed.

Before turning to the official Service-Books, a brief account of the changes that have taken place in the public worship of the Church of Scotland since 1865 may be given, but it must be remembered that they are not uniform, greater advance taking place in some districts than in others. The "Lecture" has died out and the straightforward reading of Scripture has been restored since the *Recommendation and Declaratory Act on Public Worship* (1865).[2] Organs are now common. Paraphrases were allowed in some churches from the time of their first appearance, and hymns were known in the Relief Church before the end of the eighteenth century, but it was not until the second half of the nineteenth that hymnody was taken seriously, leading up to the *Revised Church Hymnary*, 1927, "in the preparation of which all the hymn-using Presbyterian Churches of the Empire, with the exception of that of Canada, co-operated".[3] The sermon retains the central place to which Bucer and Calvin raised it. There has been a

---

[1] W. D. Maxwell, *An Outline of Christian Worship*, 1936, pp. 166–7.
[2] T. Leishman, *The Westminster Directory*, 1901, pp. xxxi–xxxii.
[3] *Revised Church Hymnary*, preface.

change of style and technique, not to speak of a change in length. The practice of "free prayer" finds continued approval; but there has been an improvement with regard to both the form and content of public prayer. Ministers are now giving more time to the study of prayer language and devotional literature.

Communion continues to be celebrated in most congregations half-yearly or quarterly, but there are cases of monthly communion, and a weekly communion is not unknown.[1] In the late nineteenth century, chiefly owing to the influence of Dr. Chalmers of St. John's Parish Church, Glasgow, and in opposition to all that the Scottish reformers and the Scottish commissioners to Westminster stood for, a change was introduced in the form of communicating, in that communicants, instead of being seated at the Table, receive the elements in the pews, which are covered with white linen "houseling cloths". There has been an improvement in church architecture. Many churches are now open each day for private prayer and meditation. There has been, also, a return to the observance of the Christian Year, and the *Book of Common Order*, 1940, supplies proper prefaces. "As a result of this slow and difficult revival," as Dr. James Moffatt says, "there is now in Scotland, a welcome variety and wealth of worship, from the simple, most impressive service of a small congregation, to the more elaborate worship in our cathedrals, abbeys, and larger churches."[2]

To sum up, this brief historical account shows:

(i) that the Reformed rite traces its ancestry through the years to the *Deutsche Messe* of Diebold Schwarz, and thence through the mediaeval Mass to the worship of the early Church and to the worship of Christ and the apostles;

(ii) that the central act of worship in the Reformed Church is the Eucharist;

(iii) that the Sunday Morning Service, arising out of a particular historical setting, ought to be based on the eucharistic norm, and that, at a later date, in a completely different historical situation this norm came to be distorted;

(iv) that proclamation of the mighty acts of God is an essential element in the Liturgy of the Word[3];

(v) that the loss of frequent communion arose from a particular historical situation;

---

[1] For the writer's comments see closing sentences of chapter VII.
[2] J. Moffatt, *The Presbyterian Churches*, 1928, p. 149.
[3] See also chapter VI.

(vi) that the loss of the Christian Year arose from State interference;

(vii) that the loss of the Creed, the Lord's Prayer, and the *Gloria Patri* arose from religious tension against an ecclesiastico-political background;

(viii) that the loss of a liturgy in the hands of the people arose from a particular politico-historical situation; and

(ix) that a bias against read prayers, Communion of the sick, and Confirmation arose for similar reasons, as did the loss of the people's "Amen" in response to prayer, which had been the common practice up to 1638.[1]

---

[1] Actually, while the writer uses the modern term "people's Amen" in the text, the people said "So be it" at the end of public prayer, but the bishops wanted them to say "Amen"; so they ended up, in opposition to the bishops, saying neither.

IV

MODERN SERVICE-BOOKS

THE WESTMINSTER *Directory for the Public Worship of God*, as approved in her Act of 1645, remains a normative standard for worship for the Church of Scotland,[1] but in 1923 *Prayers for Divine Service* was issued bearing on its title-page the words "By authority of the General Assembly of the Church of Scotland". The Church Service Society can take pride in the fact that its private and unofficial labours have resulted in an official standard of worship. In the *Euchologion* the eucharistic rite followed the preaching service, but in *Prayers for Divine Service* the Order for Holy Communion is a unified whole, being "an enriched form of the Euchologion Communion Service".[2] This is a real return to the ideals of the Reformers, although structurally Morning Prayer influenced the Liturgy of the Word in that the Creed and intercessions come before the sermon. It provides one Order for Holy Communion. The Lectionary is not based on the Christian Year, but there is, as in the *Euchologion*, a Table of Psalms and Lessons for Special Seasons, including Christmas, Good Friday, Easter, Ascension and Pentecost.

In 1929, a second edition was issued, the chief changes being that two Orders are provided for Holy Communion, and that the Lectionary is based on the Christian Year, with a Table of Lessons for Special Seasons. The first Order is basically that of the 1923 edition. In the Shorter Order the intercessions are placed in the post-communion.

This work and the *Book of Common Order*, 1928, of the United Free Church of Scotland were accepted as standards of worship at the Union of the two churches in 1929 until a new book would be prepared. In 1931 an *Ordinal and Service Book*, containing an Order for Holy Communion for use in the Courts of the Church, was published. A revised edition appeared in 1954. *Prayers for Divine Service*, 1929, and the *Book of Common Order*, 1928, were replaced by the *Book of Common Order*, 1940. This work attempted to combine the best features of its

---

[1] *Act of Union*, 1929.
[2] O. Milligan, *The Scottish Communion Office*, 1939, p. 19.

predecessors and includes much of the material supplied in them. It contains a Lectionary, based on the Christian Year, which provides an Old Testament, Epistle and Gospel. It includes prayers for the seasons of the Christian Year, and proper prefaces.

The Preface states:

> Four Orders are provided for Holy Communion. The first of them . . . closely approximates in language and arrangement to the service in the *Ordinal for use in Courts of the Church* which is now in use at the General Assembly's Communion Service. An alternative Order has been prepared for Congregations in which the more rigid traditional forms may be felt to be unsuitable; a shorter Order which is recommended for use at a second service; and a short Order for such occasions as demand brevity, as, for example, in administering Communion to the sick.

Structurally they all follow *Prayers for Divine Service* and place the intercessions in the Liturgy of the Word.

In 1935 the Church of Scotland published *Prayers for the Christian Year*, providing complete services for each of the great festivals. A second edition was issued in 1952.

A study of the English and Irish Service Books reveals that they are much indebted to all these Scottish works.

The Presbyterian Church of England revised the *Westminster Directory* in 1889, 1898 and 1921, and issued *The Presbyterian Service Book* in 1948. The preface states:

> In 1944 the Presbyterian Church of England was faced with the need for a new and revised Directory of public worship, the existing edition, published in 1921, being then out of print. At the same time the Presbyterian Church of Wales, feeling the need for a Service Book, proposed to the Presbyterian Church of England that the two General Assemblies might collaborate in the production of a book which would serve the purposes of both Churches. The English Assembly of 1944 welcomed this approach and resolved to proceed forthwith in the matter jointly with the Welsh Church. Each Assembly duly appointed members to a Joint Committee which was engaged upon its task for four years. Sanction to publish the book was granted by the Assemblies of both Churches in 1948.

The Lectionary is based on the Christian Year, and provides a psalm, Old Testament, Epistle and Gospel. It also includes prayers and services for the Christian Year. Four Orders for the celebration of Holy Communion are provided. "The first two," says the preface, "are different expressions of the Reformed tradition; the third is more in the Welsh tradition, while the fourth is a short order for use when sickness or other circumstances make an abbreviated form more desirable."

In all three Orders the intercessions are placed in the Liturgy of the Word.

The Presbyterian Church in Ireland revised the *Westminster Directory* in 1825, 1841, 1859, 1868, and 1887. A *Book of Public Worship* was first published in 1923, but only with the authority of the committee. The same applies to the 1931 edition. A revised edition was published in 1942 "By authority of the General Assembly". Each contains a Lectionary, but none of them is based on the Christian Year, although all include suggested readings and prayers for Special Seasons.

The 1923 and 1931 editions provide two Orders for Holy Communion, and the 1942 edition one, but all treat it as following the preaching service, saying, "the ordinary service should be shortened whenever it is to be followed by the observance of the Sacrament".

A new and revised edition was published "By authority of the General Assembly" in 1965. The Lectionary is taken from Table I of the *Book of Common Worship* of the Church of South India, and slightly altered, providing an Old Testament, Epistle and Gospel, a psalm, and collect of the day for each Lord's Day, as well as including special prayers for the seasons of the Christian Year, and proper prefaces.

It provides two Orders for Holy Communion. The service here is a unity consisting of the Liturgy of the Word and the Liturgy of the Faithful. The first is based on classical Reformed tradition, and is the Order recommended for use, but in the second, which had to be included because of its being common usage, the intercessions are placed in the Liturgy of the Word. An Order for Communion of the Sick is also provided.

The Reformed Church has always laid great stress on preparation for Communion and on thanksgiving afterwards. All these works contain Orders for the Service of Preparation, and the Scottish and Irish for the Thanksgiving.

When one turns to the Sunday Morning Service, the Scottish *Book of Common Order*, 1940, provides six complete Orders, in all of which the intercessions are placed before the sermon. The three Orders in the English-Welsh book follow the same pattern. In the Irish book, on the other hand, structural outlines are set out with an anthology of prayers "to prevent", as the preface says, "the book simply being opened and a Service read through without prayerful preparation". Two structural outlines are provided; the first is based on Classical Reformed practice,

39

and the second is given as an alternative "because it is in common use".

In the worship of the Reformed Church there is considerable liberty and much variety of expression. While it varies from church to church and country to country, it nevertheless is not diverse in its form. If one takes a rite from Scotland or Germany, or America or France, or Switzerland or Canada, or Italy or Brazil, and so on, and compares and contrasts it with the others, one will find a deep and real underlying unity. So for the purposes of exposition and assessment of the eucharistic rite in the Reformed Church, the writer will use the first Order for the Sacrament of the Lord's Supper in the Scottish and Irish Books, and the first and the third in the English-Welsh, as setting forth the ideals of the respective Churches in particular and the Reformed rite in general, making incidental references to other rites where necessary.

V

THE EUCHARISTIC RITE

THE EUCHARISTIC RITE in the Reformed Church is a unity consisting of the Liturgy of the Word and the Liturgy of the Faithful, so while we may divide it into sections for the sake of analysis, we must ever be mindful of this underlying, fundamental and essential unity.

The Liturgy of the Word divides into two sections, consisting of the old Liturgy of the Word derived from the synagogue, basically the proclamation of the mighty acts of God, and the later introduction, consisting of preparation to receive the Word. This is followed by the Liturgy of the Faithful, which is the response of the Faithful to the mighty acts of God, consisting of prayers for all men, a common confession of the Church's faith, and union with Christ in a rite which contains the elements of thanksgiving, commemoration, communion, sacrifice, resurrection and mystery, a rite in which Christ is really and truly present with the people of God and one of eternal and eschatological significance. Dismissal with God's blessing follows. So we have the sequence of preparation, proclamation of the mighty acts of God, response and dismissal with God's blessing, in which it has to be remembered that the preparation carries over into the proclamation, the proclamation into the response, and the response into the dismissal.

Let us now analyse these as they are set out in the Scottish, English, Welsh and Irish rites.

LITURGY OF THE WORD

Preparation

In the Scottish *Book of Common Order* the minister calls the congregation to worship, saying "Let us worship God", after which is sung a psalm or hymn, such as Psalm 43: 3–5, "O send thy light forth and thy truth."

Then follows a call to prayer in words of holy scripture, such as

What shall we render unto the Lord for all His benefits toward us? We will take the cup of salvation, and call upon the name of the Lord. We will pay our vows unto the Lord now in the presence of all His people.

41

Christ our passover is sacrificed for us; therefore let us keep the feast.

O taste and see that the Lord is good. Blessed is the man that trusteth in Him.

Sentences suitable to the seasons of the Christian Year may be substituted. This is followed by the collect for purity from the *Book of Common Prayer*, a confession of sins, supplication for pardon and love toward God, and a canticle, psalm, or hymn.

In the English rite, the service opens with the minister calling the people to prayer with the same scripture sentences as in the Scottish rite. Then follows the collect for purity, a hymn or Psalm 43: 3–5, and the same confession of sins, prayer for pardon and love towards God, as in the Scottish rite.

In the Welsh rite, the Service begins with Psalm 43: 3–5, the minister presumably saying, "Let us worship God." Then follows the scriptural sentences:

The earth is the Lord's, and the fulness thereof; the world and they that dwell therein. For He hath founded it upon the seas and established it upon the floods. Who shall ascend into the hill of the Lord, or who shall stand in His holy place? He that hath clean hands and a pure heart; who hath not lifted up his soul unto vanity, nor sworn deceitfully. He shall receive the blessing from the Lord, and righteousness from the God of his salvation.

If we confess our sins, He is faithful and just to forgive us our sins, and to cleanse us from all unrighteousness.

Then follows a prayer of confession, for pardon, of supplication, and a hymn.

In the Irish rite, the service opens with the minister saying, "Glory be to the Father, and to the Son, and to the Holy Spirit", or the scripture sentences:

In the beginning God created the heaven and the earth.

In the beginning was the Word, and the Word was with God, and the Word was God.

When the day of Pentecost was fully come, they were all with one accord in one place, and they were filled with the Holy Ghost.

Sentences suitable to the seasons of the Christian Year may be substituted.

The sentences are followed by a "Psalm or Hymn of Adoration". Then comes a prayer of confession, supplication for pardon and various graces, the collect of the day, and a supplication for illumination.

In the Scottish, English, and Welsh rites the prayer for illumination is placed before the sermon, but surely illumination is also necessary in the lections. The readings as well as the sermon, as Calvin maintained, are proclamation of the Gospel. That is why the prayer for illumination, as with Bucer and Calvin, ought to come not simply before the sermon, but before the readings and the sermon as a unity, and so within the preparation.

One's first thought in the presence of God is of his greatness and majesty, followed, in the light of this, by a recognition of one's own sinfulness and need. Calvin's service opened with the scriptural sentence, Psalm 124: 8, "Our help is in the name of the Lord who made heaven and earth." It appears, therefore, to the writer that the opening sentences in the Irish rite, together with the direction that the first singing should be one of adoration, are not only closer to Reformed tradition, but also to devotional experience, and give more adequate expression to the greatness of God than do the sentences in the Scottish and English rites.[1]

It appears also that to make the proclamation of the mighty acts of God follow a hymn as in the Scottish and Welsh rites, or the prayer of confession and supplication as in the English, does not link the preparation to the proclamation so closely as in the Irish rite, where the supplications end with a prayer for illumination.

Proclamation

In the Scottish, English and Irish rites the proclamation opens with the minister saying, "Hear the Word of God . . ." and presumably this is true also in Welsh practice.

The following is the structure of the Welsh rite:

> Lesson
> Prayer of Intercession
> Lord's Prayer
> Offering and Dedication
> Sermon

---

[1] The Scottish practice of beginning the Service with a singing is based on the "gathering psalm", which is all that now remains of the Reader's Service. As the Reader's Service was a thing distinct from the Sunday Morning Service, being a Service prefixed to it, when the *Book of Common Order*, 1940, is being revised this point should be considered.

Ascription of praise[1]
Hymn

The following is the structural outline of the English rite:
   Old Testament Reading
   Canticle, prose or metrical psalm or hymn
   New Testament Reading
   Nicene or Apostles' Creed may be said
   Prayer: Intercessions
             Thanksgiving for faithful departed
   Hymn
   Offerings and Dedication
   Prayer for illumination
   Sermon
   Ascription of praise
   Psalm or hymn

The Scottish rite has the following outline:
   Old Testament
   Psalm
   Epistle
   Gospel[2]
   Prayer: Intercessions
             Thanksgiving for faithful departed
   Psalm or hymn
   Prayer for illumination
   Sermon
   Ascription of praise
   Offerings

The Irish rite is as follows:
   Prayer for illumination (linking from preparation)
   Old Testament
   Psalm, hymn or anthem
   Epistle

[1] The writer takes it that there is a misprint in the order on p. 67 of *The Presbyterian Service Book*, 1948.

[2] The Nicene Creed is not inserted in this outline after the Gospel because, although the rubrics permit it there or after the Great Entrance, the latter position represents the normal practice.

Gospel
Psalm or hymn
Sermon, which should end with an ascription of praise
Prayer, leading into intercessions

The prayer is:

Grant, we beseech Thee, Almighty God, that Thy Word may, through Thy grace, be so grafted inwardly in our hearts, that it may bring forth in us the fruit of good living to the honour and praise of Thy holy name.

Then the minister says:

Let us make intercession unto God: Let us pray for the Church:

Several criticisms must be made here. The Scottish, English and Welsh rites have been influenced by Morning Prayer and place the intercessions within the proclamation. The sequence of thought is preparation, proclamation, and response, and the intercessions (and, in the English and Welsh rites, the offering) should not come between the readings and the sermon interrupting the flow of thought in the service by dividing the proclamation of the Word into two separate (and, unfortunately, sometimes unrelated) parts. "The lections are one and must be kept together in the service," as Dr. Dauerty says, "and the sermon is one with them, and must follow them closely."[1]

The position of the Creed in the English rite, and its permissive use in the Scottish, has the same effect. Further, while the Lectionary provides for the use of Old Testament, Epistle and Gospel, it is unfortunate that the English rite makes provision for only two lections, and the Welsh for only one.

The centrality of preaching is a feature of Reformed worship. The office of the ministry is defined in the Genevan *Ecclesiastical Ordinances* of 1541 as "that of proclaiming the Word of God".[2] The connotation of this concept will be discussed in the next chapter.

LITURGY OF THE FAITHFUL

In the liturgy of the faithful we have the response to the proclamation of the mighty acts of God. Following Dix, we may analyse it as having a fourfold structure while remaining a unity . . . Offertory, Consecration, Manual acts, and Communion. In all Reformed

---

[1] J. S. Dauerty, *Reformed Worship*, (MS., 1948), p. 55.
[2] *Ecclesiastical Ordinances*, 3.

rites, the section between the proclamation in the sermon and the Consecration appears to be the weakest, and at times quite illogical in the sequence of thought.

Up to the Offertory

Once again it is necessary to set this out structurally. It is as follows in the Welsh rite:

Creed may be said
Words of Institution as Scriptural Warrant: 1 Cor. 11: 23-26
Comfortable Words
The people may respond to this with hymn 713, "Holy, holy, holy."
The minister says:

Lift up your heads, O ye gates; and be ye lift up, ye everlasting doors: and the King of Glory shall come in. Who is this King of Glory? The Lord of hosts, He is the King of Glory.

The Lord Jesus, the same night in which He was betrayed took bread: and when he had given thanks he brake it.

According to the holy institution and example of our Lord, let us now give thanks.

Before outlining the Scottish rite, two points must be mentioned as they are fundamental in Reformed doctrine and practice.

(i) The Invitation: This is not printed in the first Order, only in the Alternative. As it is, however, a universal practice it must be mentioned. The wording is:

The Table of the Lord Jesus Christ is open to all who are in communion with the Church Universal. We therefore invite members of any branch thereof who love the Lord Jesus Christ in sincerity, to join with us in this holy fellowship.

Reformed doctrine is that the Lord's Table is not a "Reformed Table", but the "Table of the Lord". In view of this any member of Christ's Church, divided though she unfortunately is, cannot be denied the right to receive the body and blood of Christ. Its use, therefore, gives expression to the Catholicity of the Church. In passing, it may be pointed out that this is not "open communion". The invitation is addressed only to those who are communicant members of the Church.

(ii) While the text of the *Book of Common Order* does not mention it, the Invitation is followed by the "Lifting of the Tokens". Originally these tokens were made of lead, but today they are specially printed cards with texts from 1 Cor. 11, and the communicant's name and address. These are distributed to members by authority of the Kirk-Session either at the Preparation Service, or by the elders when visiting their districts. A visitor may also receive one "as a visitor" from a member of Kirk-Session on entering the church. After the Invitation these cards are lifted by the elders. This corresponds closely to the "scrutiny of the deacon" in the early Church. From this, and the wording of the Invitation, it is clear that accusations about practising "open communion" and "admitting anyone and everyone", such as have been made by Anglicans at ecumenical conferences, are quite alien to Reformed teaching and practice.

After the lifting of the tokens, the Comfortable Words are read, and during the singing of metrical Psalm 24: 7–10, the elements are brought in and placed on the Holy Table. This is followed by the Nicene Creed, after which the minister unveils the elements and offers the Offertory prayers. He then says, "The Grace of the Lord Jesus Christ be with you all," reads the Words of Institution as a scriptural warrant from 1 Cor. 11: 23–26, and says:

> Therefore, that we may fulfil His institution in righteousness and joy, let us follow His blessed example in word and action: IN THE NAME OF THE FATHER, AND OF THE SON, AND OF THE HOLY SPIRIT:

In the English rite, the minister first reads the Comfortable Words; then is sung Psalm 24: 7–10, during which the elements are brought in, or unveiled, after which he says the Offertory prayer. Then he says "The Grace", reads the warrant, and says, "Therefore, that we may fulfil . . ." as in the Scottish rite.

In order to understand the Irish revision, it is necessary here to set out the Scottish rite structurally:

Invitation
Tokens
Comfortable Words
Great Entrance, during singing of Psalm 24: 7–10
Nicene Creed, if not used earlier
Unveiling and Offertory prayers
The grace of the Lord Jesus Christ be with you all
Words of Institution: 1 Cor. 11. 23–26
Taking elements to be set apart

It appeared to the Irish committee that the Great Entrance and the Unveiling were both parts of the Offertory and so should not be separated by the Creed; further, that the Consecration should follow directly on the Offertory, the Taking to set apart being the link between the two. This meant that the Great Entrance, Unveiling, and Taking to set apart ought to come together immediately before the prayer of Consecration. There also appeared to be no reason for inserting the Grace and the Words of Institution between the Unveiling and the Taking to set apart except to separate the Offertory prayers from the prayer of Consecration. In the primitive rites there was nothing corresponding to an Offertory prayer at the moment of the Offertory, and the meaning of the Offertory was expressed in words in the Eucharistic prayer itself. The Great Entrance and Unveiling assures the concept of the Offertory as action.

Several other points also called for consideration. (i) The Comfortable Words were introduced into the *Book of Common Prayer* from the *Consultatio* of Hermann of Cologne, where they had a different significance. He used them after confession of sin and before absolution, before communicating. They make their first appearance in a Scottish Reformed rite in the *Book of Common Order*, 1928, of the United Free Church, and so came into the *Book of Common Order*, 1940. (ii) If "The Grace of the Lord Jesus Christ" were altered to "The Peace of the Lord Jesus Christ be with you all" (to which the people might respond "Amen"), it would be nearer the use of the Kiss of Peace in the early Church. (iii) The reading of the Words of Institution was held, at the Reformation, to be necessary as a scriptural warrant to show that apostolic practice was being followed, and by tradition might be retained. (iv) In the *Euchologion* of the Church Service Society the Nicene Creed was said in the form: "We believe. . . ." In *Prayers for Divine Service*, 1923, this was changed to the form: "I believe. . . ." This was felt to minimize the corporate character of the rite. The confession of faith is a confession of the Church's faith. This section of the Liturgy of the Faithful in the Irish rite is as follows:

Prayer: Intercessions
        Thanksgiving for the faithful departed
Offerings
Invitation
Comfortable Words
Psalm or Hymn, during which those not communicating may leave
Tokens
Words of Institution: 1 Cor. 11: 23–26
Nicene Creed: We believe. . . .

The Peace of the Lord Jesus Christ be with you all
Great Entrance, Unveiling, while Psalm 24: 7–10 is sung
Taking of elements to be set apart
The Invitation and Comfortable Words are addressed to all the worshippers. Tokens are then received from all who intend to communicate. The Warrant for what is about to be done is read, and confession is made of the Church's faith. To the believing community, and within it, the Peace is given. Then follows the Offertory, placed in the setting of the believing and confessing community.

The form of words for the Taking to set apart in the Irish rite differs from that in the Scottish and English rites. It is:

> The Lord Jesus, the same night in which He was betrayed took bread and wine, and gave thanks. Therefore that we may fulfil His Institution, in the Name and by the Authority of the Lord Jesus Christ, we take these elements of bread and wine to be set apart from all common uses to this holy use and mystery.

The Scottish and English rites say: "I take these elements . . ." whereas the Irish rite says: "We take. . . ." The Reformed Church has always opposed private celebration for the individual himself, and the difference here would appear to be that in the form "I take" it is an action of the minister within the Church, whereas the form "We take" makes it an action of the Church, minister and people together.

Consecration

The second action is Consecration. In the Scottish, English and Irish rites this prayer opens with the Salutation and *Sursum corda*, Preface (thanksgiving for creation and providence), the Scottish and Irish providing proper prefaces for the major Christian festivals, leading up to the *Sanctus*. All three are based on the *Liturgy of St. James*. The Welsh rite, on the other hand, opens with phraseology reminiscent of the *Sursum corda* and has a completely different thanksgiving, leading up to the *Sanctus*. In the Scottish and English rites the *Sanctus* is followed by the *Benedictus qui venit* with *Hosanna*. The joining of the *Benedictus qui venit* to the *Sanctus* arose from a conflation of texts, and is omitted in the Irish and Welsh forms.

After the *Sanctus*, in the Scottish rite, the prayer of consecration continues with:

Vere sanctus (thanksgiving for redemption)

49

Anamnesis

Oblation

Epiclesis

Self-oblation

Petition that God will fulfil in us, and all men,
His purpose of redeeming love

Doxology

Lord's Prayer

The English prayer is practically identical. The Welsh prayer, on the other hand, differs considerably. The *Sanctus* is followed by a thanksgiving for redemption, quotes Psalm 116: 12–14 (in the plural), an epiclesis, and thanksgiving for the faithful departed, omitting the Lord's Prayer.

The Irish prayer follows the Scottish form, but has several distinctive features, in that in the thanksgiving for the institution the narrative is given. This is a feature of all the early liturgies except the Nestorian, and it too may at one time have included it. This is followed by "and that after He was risen He was known to His disciples in the breaking of bread", in an attempt to give fuller expression to the Eucharist as a festival of the Resurrection.[1]

A few remarks should perhaps be added concerning the epiclesis. There was no epiclesis in the rites of Schwarz and Bucer, and it is extremely doubtful if there was one in Calvin's. The writer's opinion is that this can only be maintained by reading into *La Forme* what is not there. The same applies to the *Book of Common Order*, 1564. On the other hand, there is evidence to suggest that an epiclesis always formed part of the Scottish rite. Row[2] protests in 1622 about Patrick Galloway conducting a service without a blessing upon the elements; and Calderwood describing a Scottish Communion in 1620 says there was an epiclesis and that this had been the practice of the church for sixty years.[3]

An epiclesis was included in the Order for the Sacrament of the Lord's Supper by the Westminster Assembly. Further, at the Savoy Conference, the Presbyterians stated their objections to the *Book of Common Prayer*, 1552, in two parts, the first of which was a statement of historic Puritan objections to ceremonies, and the second a critical

---

[1] O. Cullmann, *op. cit.*
[2] J. Row, *op. cit.*, p. 338.
[3] D. Calderwood, *op. cit.*, pp. 777–8.

analysis of the Prayer Book. The first criticism was the omission of the Black rubric, and the second that, "We conceive that the manner of the consecrating of the Elements is not here explicit and distinct enough."[1] So it should be remembered that the non-inclusion of an epiclesis in the Order for Holy Communion was one of the primary reasons why Presbyterians separated from the Church of England in 1661.

It has been said that in the Reformed rite in the epiclesis "the descent of the Holy Spirit is invoked not upon the bread and wine, but on the faithful". This may be so in a few cases, for example, in France, but, broadly speaking, it is not true of the Reformed rite.

The epiclesis in the Scottish rite is as follows:

> We most humbly beseech Thee to send down Thy Holy Spirit to sanctify both us and these Thine own gifts of bread and wine which we set before Thee, that the bread which we break may be the communion of the body of Christ, and the cup of blessing which we bless the communion of the blood of Christ; that we, receiving them, may by faith be made partakers of His body and blood, with all His benefits, to our spiritual nourishment and growth in grace, and to the glory of Thy most holy name.

With regard to the epiclesis, it may be pointed out that this is not held to be the actual moment of consecration, but to give expression to the purpose of the whole prayer. The whole prayer is the prayer of consecration, and consecration is not limited or defined to a particular moment. Because of the "new theology", in the Irish rite the phrase "send down thy Holy Spirit" has been altered to "through the Holy Spirit". This avoids any suggestion that up to this the Holy Spirit was absent, being "up there".

Manual Acts

There has been a tendency to make the manual acts, breaking of bread and taking of cup, merely utilitarian, and to associate them with the delivery. The Welsh rite falls into this error. A study of the rites of the early Church, or, for that matter, of the *Westminster Directory* reveals, however, that they ought really to be a separate action, a dramatic and prophetic re-presentation of what our Lord did at the Institution. In the Scottish, English, and Irish rites the forms are substantially identical:

[1] E. Cardwell, *History of Conferences*, 1841, pp. 303–63.

The Minister shall say:

According to the holy institution, example, and command of our Lord Jesus Christ, and for a memorial of Him, we do this: who, the same night in which he was betrayed, TOOK BREAD (*here the Minister shall take the bread into his hands*), and when he had blessed, and given thanks, HE BRAKE IT (*here he shall break the bread in such a manner as to be seen by the congregation*), and said, TAKE, EAT; THIS IS MY BODY, WHICH IS BROKEN FOR YOU: THIS DO IN REMEMBRANCE OF ME.

After the same manner also, HE TOOK THE CUP (*here he shall raise the cup in such a manner as to be seen by the congregation*), saying: THIS CUP IS THE NEW COVENANT IN MY BLOOD: THIS DO YE, AS OFT AS YE DRINK IT, IN REMEMBRANCE OF ME.

Communion

As we have seen, in the Welsh rite the manual acts are associated with the delivery, so the delivery and communion follow immediately after the prayer of consecration, which does not end with the Lord's Prayer. Consequently we may study Welsh practice first.

Minister: The Lord Jesus Christ the same night in which he was betrayed TOOK BREAD: and when He had given thanks (as we have now done) HE BRAKE IT

(*here the Minister breaks the bread*)

and said,

TAKE, EAT: THIS IS MY BODY WHICH IS BROKEN FOR YOU: THIS DO IN REMEMBRANCE OF ME.

The Minister invites the people to fulfil the injunction of the Lord in some such words as;

Let us therefore eat together of this bread, and may the life which was in Him be in us as well.

Whereupon he may partake of the bread himself and, after a suitable pause, distributes it to the serving elders.

Minister:

After the same manner also HE TOOK THE CUP

(*here the Minister takes the cup into his hand*)

when He had supped, saying: THIS CUP IS THE NEW TESTAMENT IN MY BLOOD: THIS DO YE AS OFT AS YE DRINK IT, IN REMEMBRANCE OF ME.

For as often as ye eat this bread, and drink this cup, ye do show the Lord's death till He come.

The Minister then invites the people to partake of the cup in some such words as:

Let us drink together of this cup of the fellowship and may the Spirit that was in Him be in us as well.

Whereupon he may partake of the cup himself and, after a suitable pause, serves the elders.

When the elders are ready, the Minister shall deliver the bread to them, and subsequently the wine, that they may serve the people.

In the other rites, the manual acts are followed by the *Agnus Dei* and the delivery and communion. The form of delivery is substantially the same in all three, so the writer quotes only the Irish rite:

The Minister shall serve himself, receive in both kinds, then distribute to the elders and those assisting him and to the congregation, saying:
Distribution of the Bread:
TAKE, EAT, This is the body of Christ, which is broken for you: This do in remembrance of Him.
Distribution of the Cup:
DRINK YE ALL OF IT, This cup is the new covenant in the blood of Christ, which is shed for you: This do in remembrance of Him.

A few features in Reformed practice require further treatment here.

(i) The celebrant in the Reformed Church must be a Minister of the Word, and always adopts the basilican position.

(ii) In the British Isles, the normal mode is for communicants to receive sitting in the pews. This is a change from earlier custom, because formerly communicants left the pews, singing Psalm 116: 13–19, "I'll of salvation take the cup", and took their seats at a long "table in the aisles". A few congregations in Scotland and Ireland still retain this practice. The change was received from English Puritanism, through Congregationalism and Anglicanism. Pusey used this form in Christ Church, Oxford, as late as 1856, and it was still the custom in Trinity College, Cambridge, in 1870. It was first introduced into Scotland in St. John's Church, Glasgow, in 1824. Although condemned by the General Assembly in 1825, it appealed to many because it reduced the length of the service, and it is now the general practice. On the Continent, practice varies. In Holland and Wesphalia, for example, they still use the "Table in the aisles"; whereas in France, Alsace and Switzerland, the communicants come forward and receive standing, not at an altar-rail, but around the Table.

(iii) As it is customary for elders to carry the bread and wine to those communicating in the pews, a word of explanation is necessary. The Minister is the celebrant, and the elders are simply the Minister's arms extended. They are deacons. This function, however, may be performed by any communicant member at the request of the Minister, although it is customary for the elders to do so. The Minister, and he alone, is the celebrant, under Christ.[1]

(iv) In many places the "individual" cup has been substituted for the "common" cup, and "unfermented wine" for hock, sherry, claret and port.

Conclusion

In the early Church the people were quickly dismissed after communicating, but later a conclusion was added to the service.

In the Welsh rite this consists of a prayer of thanksgiving and of self-dedication, the receiving of a communion offering, a hymn, and the benediction. All that it is necessary to say here is that Dix has shown that the placing of the self-dedication in the post-communion when there is no self-oblation in the Anaphora tends towards Zwinglianism.[2]

The English rite is as follows:

> Pax
> Prayer: Thanksgiving
>   Union with the faithful departed
> Psalm, hymn, or Nunc dimittis
> Benediction: The peace of God, which passeth all understanding. . . .

The Scottish rite is structurally identical, providing three alternative thanksgivings, the first from the Book of Common Prayer and the third based on the Book of Common Order, 1564; and instead of the emphasis being on "union with the departed" it is for "grace to follow them as they followed Christ", and that "with them" we may be brought "to those things which eye hath not seen, nor ear heard, which Thou has prepared for them that love Thee".

The Irish rite links the Peace with the Creed, as was true of the Kiss of Peace in the early Church, and so omits it here, substituting an ascription of praise:

Now unto the God of all grace, who hath called us unto His eternal glory by Christ Jesus, be glory and dominion for ever and ever.

This is followed by two prayers, one of thanksgiving to God, Father, Son, and Holy Spirit; and the other looking to the coming of

---

[1] H. Heyer, L'Église de Genève, 1909, pp. 270, 285-6. WCF, 27: 4; 29: 3.
[2] G. Dix, op. cit., pp. 640-74.

Christ in glory. Then comes a psalm or hymn of thanksgiving: a dismissal, "Go forth in the peace of Christ to serve Him in the world", linking worship and service; and the apostolic benediction.

Thanksgiving for Communion is so important in the Reformed Church that it is the practice in all these Churches to hold special Thanksgiving Services after Communion, and the Scottish and Irish Service-Books provide Orders for such services.

VI

THE SUNDAY MORNING SERVICE

WE HAVE SEEN how the Sunday Morning Service in the Reformed Church came into being, and that it ought to be based on the eucharistic norm. The sequence of ideas is preparation (the greatness and majesty of God, man's sinfulness and need), proclamation of the mighty acts of God, and response. We have also seen how the Scottish and English rites have been influenced by Anglican Morning Prayer in the Liturgy of the Word, and so this needs only to be summarized here. In the first Order in the English Service-Book, the Lord's Prayer is placed after the supplications; and the Apostles' Creed, prayer of thanksgiving and intercession, and the offering and dedication are placed between the New Testament reading and the sermon, thus interrupting the unity of the proclamation. The service ends:

> Ascription of praise
> Hymn
> Prayer
> *Nunc dimittis*
> Salutation
> Benediction

In the first Order, in the Scottish rite, the Apostles' Creed and prayer of thanksgiving, intercession, and Lord's Prayer are placed between the Gospel and the sermon. Here, also, the proclamation is interrupted. In the Scottish rite the service, after the sermon, continues:

> Ascription of praise
> Offerings and Dedication
> Psalm, paraphrase or hymn
> Benediction

In the Scottish and English books the services are set out in full. The Irish book, on the other hand, sets out a structural outline Order of Service, and provides an anthology of prayers from which the Minister may make a selection.

As the Irish rite structurally approximates more closely than the others to the eucharistic norm, the first Order of Service may be given in full:

ORDER OF SERVICE

Preparation
 Scriptural Sentences
 Psalm or Hymn of Adoration
 Prayer: Confession OR Adoration
     Pardon   Confession
     Supplication   Pardon
             Supplication
 Psalm or Hymn (omitted if only four singings)
 Prayer: Collect of the Day
     Illumination

The Word of God
 O.T. Reading
 Psalm, Hymn, or Anthem
 N.T. Readings: Epistle
        Gospel
 Psalm or Hymn
 Sermon

Response to the Word
 Prayer: Intercessions OR Thanksgiving
     Thanksgiving for   Intercessions
      faithful departed Thanksgiving for faithful
     Lord's Prayer   departed
             Lord's Prayer

 Apostles' Creed may be said
 Offering
 Prayer: Thanksgiving OR Dedication of self and gifts
     Dedication of self
      and gifts
 Psalm or Hymn of Thanksgiving

Dismissal with God's Blessing
 Dismissal
 Apostolic Benediction

Before proceeding to discuss the meaning of the "Word of God" and the relationship of "Word" and "Sacrament" in Reformed theology, the writer would make a few general remarks about (i) psalmody and hymnody, (ii) forms of prayer, (iii) creed, offering and dedication, and (iv) the dismissal and benediction.

One of the characteristics of the Calvinistic reform was the use of metrical psalmody and the psalter still in use in Scotland is the General Assembly's revision of the Westminster psalter. The Presbyterian Church in Ireland authorized a revised psalter in 1880. To psalmody, paraphrases and hymns have since been added. It is with the structure of the Hymnal, not its contents, the writer wishes to deal. The present hymnal, the *Revised Church Hymnary*, published in 1927, and used in the Scottish, English, Irish, Welsh, and other Churches, sets out the contents on a doctrinal basis. However, examination shows that this was not very successful. The preparation of a new book is in progress. In this, a brilliant suggestion was put forward by the Rev. Stewart Todd, Edinburgh, "Why not base the contents on the Order of Service?" This was adopted, and while it has not been finalized the general structure should be along something like the following lines:

I The Humble Approach to God
    1. Approach:
        (a) for general use
        (b) for occasional use
    2. Confession and Supplication
    3. Illumination
II The Word of God: The Mighty Acts of God
    1. Creation and Providence
    2. Salvation in Jesus Christ
        (a) His Incarnation
        (b) His Life and Ministry
        (c) His Cross and Passion
        (d) His Resurrection and Ascension
        (e) His Reign and Priesthood
        (f) His Coming with power
    3. The Gift of the Holy Spirit
        (a) Pentecost
        (b) The Holy Spirit in the Church
III Response to the Word of God
    1. Adoration, Thanksgiving, and Affirmation
    2. Intercession, Service, and Witness
    3. Dedication and Stewardship
    4. The Church Triumphant
IV The Sacraments of the Church

    1. Holy Baptism
    2. The Lord's Supper
V The Ordinances of the Church
    1. Confirmation
    2. Ordination

This is as much as it is necessary to outline for our purpose here. This is bound to be a tremendous benefit in churches which have not a liturgy in the hands of the people as it will place, at least, the structural sequence of thought in the service therein and familiarize the people therewith.

In 1932 the Church of Scotland published a pamphlet entitled *A Year's Praise*, in which was set out selected praise including a gradual psalm for each Sunday of the Christian Year. In the third edition (1958) references to suitable anthems from the *Oxford Easy Anthem Book* were added. The use of this pamphlet along with the scheme of the new hymnal, when it is completed, can only bring enrichment and a deeper understanding of the meaning of worship.

Secondly, with regard to prayer, it may be pointed out that this may be offered according to various forms: prayer said by the minister in the name of the congregation, common prayer (by which the writer means prayers repeated together), responsive prayer, and silent prayer. One of the greatest weaknesses in the Reformed tradition is that prayer in public worship has been almost completely limited to the first form. This means that other forms, which give expression to the sense of fellowship and oneness, are neglected. Admittedly all the Service-Books we are specially studying provide for various forms, but unfortunately they are not so widely used as they might be. In view of the Reformers' ideal that worshippers should actively participate in the act of worship there can be no real objection to their use. Further, it is a vital necessity to use them as many young people, having become accustomed to prayer in various forms in school, feel that prayer in church has no real meaning for them.

Thirdly, in the early days of the Reformed Church the Tables were never "furnished" before the Liturgy of the Faithful, and the practice in Strasbourg, Geneva, and Scotland was to bring the bread and wine to the Holy Table immediately following the Creed, that is within the community which had confessed its faith. At the Sunday Morning Service, when the Eucharist is not celebrated, but Ante-Communion, the offering should be seen in the same context, that is, of the confessing community. In the offering we do not offer ourselves and our gifts as individuals, we offer ourselves and our gifts as members of the body of Christ, as members of a confessing community. So the Creed, offering, and prayer of thanksgiving and dedication of ourselves and our substance should be seen as closely linked.

Fourthly, with regard to the Dismissal and Benediction, it may be said that the former is of value in so far as a challenge to service of Christ in the world is presented to the people. This is followed by the Benediction, for they must never be dismissed and sent forth in their own strength, but "in the name of the Lord", having God's blessing upon them.

Let us now turn to a consideration of the connotation of the term "Word of God" in Reformed theology. When we speak of the "Word of God" and of the "Ministry of the Word", we must try to understand what is meant by these terms. It does not mean the Ministry of the Bible, but the Ministry of the Gospel of Christ. While individual sentences may be quoted from all the Reformers, including Calvin, which appear to identify the scriptures and the Word of God, this is not true of their teaching taken as a whole; for example, the Westminster *Shorter Catechism* says, "The Word of God which is contained in the scriptures of the Old and New Testaments," but further states, "The Spirit of God maketh the reading" and "preaching of the word effectual".[1] The Holy Spirit makes the written word the Living Word. "Word and Spirit", says Calvin, "both must be present if the sovereignty of God is to be established."[2] And again, "For as the all-sufficient testimony of God is contained in His word, the latter does not find the response of human faith until it is sealed by the inner witness of the Holy Spirit."[3] Reformed theology does not confuse but distinguishes the ONE WORD and the words of scripture, Jesus Christ the soul of the Bible and the extant written message which bears witness to Him. Professor Niesel sums it up:

> Calvin . . . does not forget that the Holy Spirit, which is the Spirit of Christ, stands wholly in the service of God's self-revelation. The task of the Spirit is to make us sensitive to the one Word which lies concealed in the words of Scripture; it must therefore use the written words and quicken them for our understanding. In order to bring the incarnate Word near to us the Spirit needs the written word, and proves itself as the Holy Spirit, the third Person of the Trinity, by respecting the testimony which prophets and apostles bear to the historical revelation of God in Jesus Christ. He does not speak other-

[1] *Shorter Catechism*, 2; 89.
[2] *CR*, xlv, 197.
[3] *Institutes*, i, 7, 4; i, 8, 13; *CR*, xxxix, 42.

wise today than as He once spoke through those men of old, He testifies to Jesus Christ, and thus we must await the action of the Holy Spirit from no other source but that of the Biblical witness. These considerations should make it clear that Calvin's opinions about the relation of Word and Spirit are governed by the insight that the one theme of Holy Scripture is the incarnate Word itself.[1]

So the Word is Christ, and the ministry of the Word is the ministry of Christ, or of the Gospel of Christ.

The reading and preaching of the Word are both proclamation. In the Reformed rite the sermon is considered to be an integral and essential part in any act of worship. Indeed, the sermon has a "sacramental" significance as therein God deals with man as a reasoning being. It should be based on the lections, and is a showing forth of the incarnation, life, and death of Jesus Christ, and the power of His resurrection, that He may be glorified, worshipped and served.

Thus, Professor T. F. Torrance says:

Kerygma means both the thing preached and the preaching of it in one. It is the proclamation of the Christ-event, but such proclamation that by the Holy Spirit it becomes the actualization of that event among men. It is such proclamation that in and through it the living Christ continues to do and to teach what He had already begun before and after the crucifixion. Kerygma is the Word of the Kingdom that cannot be conveyed in mere speech, but is used by God to intervene Himself in the human situation as He who once and for all has wrought out His final act in the death and resurrection of Jesus Christ, so that through kerygma the Church is continually being called out of history to become the very Body of Christ, and by the communion of His Holy Spirit is given to taste the powers of the age to come and to stand already on the side of the resurrection. . . . This means that kerygma is in the fullest sense the sacramental action of the Church through which the mystery of the Kingdom concerning Christ and His Church, hid from the foundation of the world, is now being revealed in history. Just as in the Incarnation the Word was made flesh, so in kerygma the same Word continues to be "made flesh" in the life of the Church.[2]

The Reformed Church refuses to make a qualitative distinction between the grace exhibited or mediated by the Word and that exhibited or mediated by the Sacraments. It conjoins Word and Sacrament, as both given by the Lord of the Church, the Sacrament "sealing" what

---

[1] W. Niesel, *Theology of Calvin*, 1956, p. 39. Surely "it" and "itself" should be "he" and "himself".

[2] T. F. Torrance, *Conflict and Agreement in the Church*, 1960, ii, 158–9.

the Word proclaims. As a matter of experience, she would recognize certain differences on the subjective side between listening to the Word and receiving the Sacrament, but because of her objective assimilation of Word and Sacrament she would tend to reduce the subjective experiential difference to a minimum. She would consider the grace of God in the Sacrament to inhere not in the nature of the sacramental acts *per se*, but in the action of Christ, who Himself is for her both the Word and Sacrament of God.

Turning to the relationship of the Word to the Sacraments, we find that in Reformed theology instead of speaking of the Word (Gospel) and the Sacraments it is more correct to speak of the Gospel and the Sacraments of the Gospel. Worship rests upon a doctrinal basis, and so worship may be said to be belief come to life. Dr. H. G. Hageman writes:

> The . . . Catechism tells about the atoning death of Christ; the Lord's Supper shows it forth; a sermon proclaims the presence of Christ with His people; the Holy Communion actualizes it. A Confession of faith declares that God always takes the initiative in Man's salvation; the Sacrament of Infant Baptism demonstrates it.[1]

Reformed theology holds that Jesus Christ in His birth and life, and death and resurrection worked in His human nature all that was necessary for the salvation of mankind. "What we constantly maintain", says Calvin, "is that our righteousness and life are in the death and resurrection of Christ."[2] "Having become with us the son of man, He has made us with Himself sons of God. . . ."[3] Thus there is between Christ and ourselves, through His incarnation, and death and resurrection, what Calvin calls a "holy brotherhood".[4] So Calvin speaks of the sacraments as being signs and seals of our incorporation in the body of Christ. He says:

> Baptism is an engrafting into the body of Christ, for God in that ordinance does not represent anything but what He is prepared to accomplish, provided we are on our part capable of it. The apostle, also, observes here a most admirable medium in teaching that the nature of baptism is to connect us with Christ's body.[5]

[1] *Theology Today*, 1949, p. 500.
[2] *Institutes*, iii. 11. 12.
[3] *Ibid.*, iv. 17. 2; *CR*, xxxv, 600, 602–03, 653.
[4] *Institutes*, ii. 12. 2.
[5] 1 Cor. 12: 13; *CR*, xlix, 501–02.

The Lord's Supper is equally with baptism a sign and seal of this same mystical incorporation in the body of Christ. Calvin says:

> The signs are bread and wine which represent the invisible food which we receive from the body and blood of Christ. For as God, regenerating us in baptism, ingrafts us into the fellowship of the Church, and makes us His by adoption, so . . . He performs the office of a provident parent in continually supplying the food by which He may sustain and preserve us in the life into which He has begotten us by His Word.[1]

In the Lord's Supper "we are ingrafted into the Lord's body".[2] It "is a help by which we may be ingrafted into the body of Christ, or, already ingrafted, may be more and more united to Him, until the union is completed in heaven".[3]

This union in Him is the work of the Holy Spirit,[4] and is the basis of the Church.[5] Calvin sees both sacraments as having the same end, namely, to testify and to assist in effecting our union with the body of Christ.[6]

Professor T. F. Torrance sums up the relation of the Word and Sacraments, as follows:

> It is important to remember that both Baptism and Eucharist are sacraments of the Word made flesh. They do not have existence or reality independently of the Word. To make them self-sufficient and independent of the Word would be to take away their sacramental character, for it would deny to them their element of mystery, or infinite recession in the Word that is in the bosom of God and is God. That is why, following St. Augustine, the Reformers insisted that it is the Word which sacramentalizes, and apart from the Word sacraments cannot exist. Apart from the Word there is only an empty sign that is nothing but a ceremony. *Kergyma* and sign go together and cannot be sundered. In *kerygma* the *Word* is made flesh. In the sacraments the Word is made *flesh*. Baptism, *kerygma*, and Eucharist together form a whole, the sacramental life and action of the Church.[7]

It is essential for a true understanding of Reformed rites to grasp the connotation of the term "Word of God", and to recognize that the

---

[1] *Institutes*, iv. 17. 1.
[2] I Cor. 10: 15; *Institutes*, iv. 17. 33; *CR*, xlix, 463.
[3] *Institutes*, iv. 17. 33; *CR*, xlviii, 594.
[4] Heb. 10: 29; *Institutes*, iv. 17. 10; *CR*, lv, 136.
[5] Titus 3: 5; *Institutes*, iv. 17. 8; *CR*, ix, 114–15; xxxvii, 58, 269; lii, 430.
[6] Deut. 7: 19–24; *Institutes*, iv. 18. 19; *CR*, xxvi, 564; xlv, 710; xlvii, 422.
[7] T. F. Torrance, *op. cit.*, ii, 164–5.

sacramental activity of the Church must not be exalted over the Word, for neither can be ultimately separated from the other.

Reformed theology emphasizes the inseparability of the Word of God, the Sacraments, and Faith. All are Divine in origin. Faith, as the *Heidelberg Catechism* puts it, proceeds "from the Holy Spirit, who works in our hearts by the preaching of the Gospel, and confirms it by the use of the sacraments".[1] The efficacy of the Word is a result of the faith of the hearers, and of the Sacrament of the Lord's Supper of the faith of the partakers. This faith is a gift of God. Thus the efficacy of the Word and/or the Lord's Supper can and must be reduced to the goodness of God. On the other hand, if one takes the sacramental *signa* without faith, one cannot blame the faithful God for their inefficacy, because this inefficacy is due to one's own sin, to one's failure to respond to the love of God proclaimed in Christ through the Holy Spirit. Through God's gift of Faith the Word and Sacraments have their efficacy. Wotherspoon and Kirkpatrick say:

> Faith is . . . required for our assimilation of all the blessings that the Sacraments convey. Faith is the correspondence of the human will with the Divine action. To come in faith to a Sacrament is to come to it ENTIRELY, soul as well as body: the soul seeking it, grasping it, yielding to it, apprehending it in its spiritual part, as the body apprehends and receives its outward part or sign. The whole man then comes to a whole Sacrament.[2]

[1] *Heidelberg Catechism*, 65; *Second Helvetic Confession*, 19.
[2] H. J. Wotherspoon and J. M. Kirkpatrick, *A Manual of Church Doctrine*, ed. T. F. Torrance and R. S. Wright, 1960, p. 20.

VII

THEOLOGY IN THE EUCHARISTIC RITE

IN THE Apostles' Creed and the Nicene is summed up the doctrine of the Church Catholic. Indeed, the Westminster divines described the former as "a brief sum of the Christian faith, agreeable to the word of God, and anciently received in the churches of Christ".[1] They are based on the Trinitarian formula: "in the name of the Father, and of the Son, and of the Holy Spirit".

The first article, on the Father, has been expanded to set forth God as All-sovereign, Creator and Father; the second, on the Son, to set forth the six redemptive acts of Christ: born, crucified, risen, ascended, reigning, and coming again to judge the living and the dead; and the third, on the Holy Spirit, to set forth the three principal works of the Spirit: in the Church, in forgiveness, and in eternal life.

We have now to ask: do the Reformed rites bear witness to these truths? The Irish rite in the ascription of glory certainly places God, Father, Son, and Holy Spirit, right at the centre of worship as it opens; or, if the scripture sentences are used, the fact that God is the Lord of creation, that Christ was in the beginning with His redemptive purpose, and that the Holy Spirit is creative of the Church is emphasized. The Welsh sentences also emphasize that "the earth is the Lord's" and that He is a saving God, who "is faithful and just to forgive us". On the other hand, the Scottish and English rites emphasize rather God's redemptive purpose with "Christ our passover is sacrificed for us". All four rites in the confession of sin see it as sin against "the Father" and in the prayer for pardon ask a Father's forgiveness. The Welsh rite, in addition, in the prayer of supplication refers to the assembled congregation as "we, thy children".

In all four rites the Christian Year is followed; so in the lections and sermon the mighty acts of God as Creator, Father, Preserver and Upholder are set forth. The same is true where psalms and hymns are linked to the Christian Year. God's Fatherhood is held forth in the Lord's Prayer. In the prayer of intercession (no text is given in the

[1] *Shorter Catechism.*

65

Welsh rite) God is seen as Father and Ruler of the Church, of the nations, of ministers, teachers, doctors, administrators, of the sick, the young and the aged. The needs of mankind are met only in Him. That He is "Father Almighty, Maker of heaven and earth, and of all things visible and invisible" is confessed in the Creed. The Anaphora in the Welsh rite opens,

> O God, our heavenly Father, we, Thine unworthy children, praise and bless Thy holy name for the majesty of Thy glory and for all Thy wondrous works,

and the Scottish and Irish rites,

> It is verily meet, right, and our bounden duty, that we should at all times and in all places give thanks unto Thee, O Holy Lord, Father Almighty, Everlasting God; who didst create the heavens and the earth and all that is therein; who didst make man in Thine own image and whose tender mercies are over all Thy works.

The same concept, omitting the specific reference to the creation of man, is to be found in the English Anaphora. The post-communions also in all four rites set forth the sovereignty of God, as do the benedictions.

The redemptive purpose of God in Christ is clearly set forth in all four rites, the six redemptive acts being witnessed to in the Creed and in the Anaphora, both in the thanksgiving for redemption and in the anamnesis; and also in the proper prefaces in the Scottish and Irish books. In all, forgiveness is sought "through Jesus Christ our Lord". The same is true of the supplications; only through Christ can grace and gifts be supplied to sinful man. In the lections and sermon His redemptive work is proclaimed. Only through Christ can the needs of mankind be met in the intercessions. The redemptive work of Christ is specially held forth in the Offertory prayers in the Scottish and English rites, and in all in the Creed, the Warrant, the Anaphora, the *Agnus Dei* (omitted in the Welsh), and in the words of distribution. In the Irish rite special emphasis is placed on the second coming in the second post-communion:

> Almighty and everlasting God, before whom stand the spirits of the living and the dead, we, who this day have partaken of the body and blood of Christ, rejoicing in the communion of saints, praise Thee for the assurance that we, with them, may be partakers of Thy heavenly kingdom at the coming of our Lord Jesus Christ in glory; to whom, with Thee, and the Holy Spirit, be all glory and praise, world without end.

The doctrine of the Holy Spirit is witnessed to in the Creed, and also in the lections and sermon. Also, it may be assumed that the underlying belief in all prayers for guidance is that they are answered through the Spirit.

The Irish Order opens with the scriptural sentence Acts 2: 1 and 4a, "They were all filled with the Holy Ghost", placing the rite in the setting of Pentecost, and witnessing to the Holy Spirit as creative of the Church. All four rites testify to the sanctifying power of the Holy Spirit in the epiclesis. The Scottish, English, and Irish rites contain the collect for purity from the *Book of Common Prayer*, and the last also gives the collect for charity. In the prayer for forgiveness the Scottish and English rites say, "Deliver us by Thy Holy Spirit." The Irish rite contains the words: "Let us pray for the illumination of the Holy Spirit in the reading and preaching of the Gospel." Here the Holy Spirit is seen as the bestower of gifts. The Irish rite in the intercessions refers to the Holy Spirit in connection with the Church's life and the work of healing; in the post-communion, says, "Glory, thanks, and praise be to the Spirit, holy and eternal, the Lord and Giver of Life"; and ends with the apostolic benediction, saying, "the communion of the Holy Spirit, be with you all".

With regard to Catholic doctrine, therefore, we may say that this is clearly set forth in Reformed rites, but perhaps the *caveat* should be made that, while the doctrine of the Father and that of the Son are adequately set forth, witnessing to the doctrine of the Holy Spirit requires fuller expression.

Without attempting a full outline of evangelical doctrine, as set out in the Catechisms and Confessions of the Reformation period, it may be said that it centred on (a) the sole Headship of Christ in His Church, (b) the primacy of scriptural authority, (c) salvation by grace and justification by faith, and (d) the priesthood of believers.

We have now to ask how far the Reformed rites bear witness to these doctrines. The doctrinal standards underlying worship hold these forth, and they are also proclaimed in the Word read and preached.

(a) With regard to the first, it is hardly necessary to say that in none of the Liturgies is the Pope spoken of as the head of the Church. Neither is prayer made to saints. In all, prayer, praise and adoration are addressed to God "through" or "in the name of" Christ. In the intercessions in the Irish rite the prayer for the Church opens, "Grant, O Lord God, that Thy Church, as it hath one Foundation and one Head . . ." and in the English rite, "O God, who art the hope of all the ends of the earth; we pray for Thy Holy Catholic Church, which Thou hast called. . . ." In the Creed He is proclaimed as a King "whose Kingdom shall have no end".

There is the further point that what is done is done "in the name of Christ"; for example, in the Scottish, English, and Irish rites, the Taking to set apart is "That we may fulfil His institution". Again in the Baptismal service the three books proclaim the candidate is now received into the membership of the Church "According to Christ's commandment". In the Confirmation rites, also, in the Scottish and Irish books the candidate is admitted "in the name of the Lord Jesus Christ", the Scottish adding, "the great King and Head of the Church". The same remarks are true of the Ordinal and the Marriage services. Indeed, while the formula may not be specifically repeated, every act of worship is "in the name of Christ, the sole King and Head of the Church".

(b) When we speak of the primacy of scriptural authority, it must not be taken to mean that the Reformed Church gives no place to tradition. The relation of scripture and tradition was expressed by the sixteenth General Council of the World Presbyterian Alliance, as follows:

> In liturgy, as in doctrine, the Reformed Church recognizes as normative— as absolutely binding—only what is revealed by the word of God contained in our Bible (*scriptura sola*). In liturgy, as in doctrine, the Reformed Church cannot recognize tradition as a second normative authority alongside the Bible. Therefore she admits variety of liturgical forms in everything that is not fixed by scripture. But, in liturgy as in doctrine, the Reformed Church respects tradition as a consultative authority. Her liberty in all that is not fixed by the word of God permits her therefore to preserve or to recover all traditional elements that are not clearly anti-evangelical. (She is favourably disposed towards tradition, until compelled to dissent by proof to the contrary because her aim is not to be anti-catholic but pro-evangelical.)[1]

The centrality of Scripture is evident from the provision of Lectionaries, and the insistence on the reading and preaching (based on the lections) as an essential element in the liturgy of the Word. This is also clearly seen in that scriptural authority is necessary to every Ordinance, and that no Sacrament or Ordinance should be celebrated without reading and preaching of the Word. A further evidence of the witness to scriptural authority is in the use made in the Sacraments of Scriptural Warrants.

(c) That salvation is by grace and justification by faith in Christ

[1] *Report and Proceedings*, 1948, pp. 212–13.

alone is clearly set forth in the catechisms and confessions and is an integral element in the sermon. What has already been stated about witness to Christ under Catholic doctrine is also relevant here. That forgiveness and newness of life come from Christ is clearly set forth in the prayers for forgiveness. The Welsh rite is, "Have mercy upon us, most merciful Father, for the sake of Jesus Christ, Thy Son and our Lord, and forgive us. . . ." The Scottish and English rites have with slight differences in punctuation, "Yet now, most merciful Father, have mercy upon us; for the sake of Jesus Christ, forgive us all our sins . . .", whereas the Irish rite is, "Grant unto us pardon, absolution, and remission from all our sins; confirm and strengthen us in all goodness, and bring us to eternal life; through Jesus Christ our Lord." In the Creed is proclaimed the truth that Jesus Christ was born "for us men and for our salvation". In the Anaphora in the Scottish and English rites the anamnesis reads, "Wherefore, having in remembrance the work and passion of our Saviour Christ, and pleading His eternal sacrifice. . . ."

(d) The doctrine of the priesthood of believers is undoubtedly set forth in confessional statements and sermons. That the Reformed rites bear witness to this is evident in that prayer is addressed to God "through" or "in the name of" Christ. Commenting on the meaning of this usage, Dr. C. F. D. Moule writes,

Prayer to God in the name of Christ implies that worshippers may now approach into the very presence of the Almighty with new confidence because the death of Christ has torn the separating curtain which hitherto had excluded from direct approach. In this sense, Christ's own "flesh" is a new way into the presence of God—a way which is "alive", for the way is the living Christ: incorporate in His humanity our humanity now enters the presence of God (Heb. 10: 20). Or again, it implies that, although personally unworthy, we are able to return into the family of God because of the costly forgiveness offered by God Himself and put into effect in the death of Christ: God in Christ has reconciled us; therefore it is through Christ that we draw near. Or yet again, it is the same Spirit of God who in Jesus of Nazareth cried, "Abba! Father!" (the cry of absolute obedience) who now cries "Abba! Father!" in us; so that it is "through Christ" that the Holy Spirit works in our wills enabling us to draw near to God (Mark 14:26; Rom. 8: 15; Gal. 4: 6).[1]

Cursory though this discussion of Evangelical doctrine is, it is evident that the Reformed rites do set it forth in worship.

[1] C. F. D. Moule, *Worship in the New Testament*, 1961, p. 71.

The meaning of "Word of God" and of the relationship of "Word" and "Sacrament" in Reformed theology have already been discussed in Chapter VI; so, when we turn to particular doctrine, it is sufficient to discuss the doctrine of the Eucharist. Professor T. L. Haitjema says:

> In the doctrine of the Sacraments the Reformed Churches know that they have to think in the sphere of the Holy Spirit, that is to say, in the sphere of the Church after Pentecost in which all institutions and forms and acts are dead and empty and powerless, unless the Holy Spirit comes and makes all alive and full of blessing through His Majesty. The Holy Spirit will use the preaching of the Gospel and the performance of the Sacraments as His instruments for building up and strengthening faith in believers.[1]

The aim of Baptism and the Lord's Supper is that the faith of believers may be strengthened; so the doctrine of the sacraments has to be explained in the light of the *sola fides*.

Sacramental doctrine in the Reformed Church rejects both an "untenable materialism" and a "bare symbolism". The *Scots Confession*, 1560, says, "We utterly condemn the vanity of those that affirm Sacraments to be nothing else but naked and bare signs";[2] and the Westminster catechisms condemn a "carnal" interpretation.[3] The term "symbol" in Reformed theology is used, not in the popular but in its biblical sense, as constituting an act of God in the sacrament. It is not a symbol of things absent, but of things present. The Reformed Church proclaims in the Eucharist the real presence of Christ with His Church, but this is not defined in terms of the bread and wine. He is personally present in the whole rite, and believers outwardly receiving the visible elements do really and spiritually, not carnally, partake of His body and blood. Concerning the bread and wine the *Scots Confession* says,

> We confess and undoubtedly believe that the faithful, in the right use of the Lord's Table, do so eat the body and drink the blood of the Lord Jesus that He remaineth in them and they in Him; yea, they are so made flesh of His flesh, and bone of His bone, that as the eternal Godhead hath given to the flesh of Christ Jesus life and immortality, so doth Christ, by His flesh and blood, eaten and drunken by us, give us the same prerogatives.[4]

[1] A. C. Headlam and R. Dunkerley (ed.), *The Ministry and the Sacraments*, 1937, p. 166. Knowing Professor T. L. Haitjema, the writer feels sure that, had English been his first language, for "performance" he would have used either "celebration" or more probably "administration".

[2] *Scots Confession*, 21.

[3] *Shorter Catechism*, 96; *Larger Catechism*, 170.

[4] *Scots Confession*, 21.

The *Westminster Confession* says that Christians receive Christ "by faith, really and indeed, yet not carnally and corporally . . . in, with, or under the bread and wine, yet . . . spiritually".[1]

Consequently, in the *Westminster Directory*, the minister is to pray that God "may vouchsafe His gracious presence, and the effectual working of His Spirit in us; and so to sanctify these elements both of bread and wine, and to bless His own ordinance, that we may receive by faith the body and blood of Jesus Christ crucified for us".[2]

This is the significance of the epiclesis in the Scottish, English, Irish, and Welsh rites.

The doctrine of transubstantiation was an attempt to give expression to a truth, namely, the real presence of Christ. While we must reject its "crude materialism", yet we must be careful in doing so not to reject, but to safeguard, the underlying truth of Christ's presence with His people in the celebration of the Eucharist.

The Reformed Church emphasizes the inseparability of the Word of God, the Sacraments, and Faith. That it is real reception of the body and blood of Christ, through faith, is evident from the wording of the epiclesis in the Scottish, English, and Irish rites: "That we, partaking of them, may receive by faith the body and blood of Jesus Christ."

That it is a real reception of the body and blood of Christ is clear also from the words of distribution:

Take, eat; this is the body of Christ, which is broken for you: this do in remembrance of Him.

This cup is the new covenant in the blood of Christ; which is shed for many unto remission of sins: drink ye all of it.

The devotional meaning of the Lord's Supper is that this Sacrament, which assures to the faithful the benefits purchased by Christ, has for its purpose "their spiritual nourishment and growth in Him, their further engagement in and to all duties which they owe unto Him; and to be a bond and pledge of their communion with Him, and with each other, as members of His mystical body".[3]

The Anaphora in the Scottish, English, and Irish rites prays that we may be partakers of the body and blood of Christ "to our spiritual nourishment and growth in grace". This is followed by the self-oblation and the prayer:

[1] *WCF*, 29: 7.
[2] T. Leishman, *The Westminster Directory*, 1901, pp. 50–51.
[3] *WCF*, 29: 1.

We beseech thee mercifully to accept this our sacrifice of praise and thanksgiving, as in fellowship with all thy faithful in heaven and on earth, we pray thee to fulfil in us, and in all men, the purpose of Thy redeeming love.

While this too has been a cursory survey, we may conclude that the Reformed doctrine of the Eucharist is faithfully set forth in these rites.

This leaves three further matters to be discussed, namely, Reservation, Communion of the sick, and Frequency of Communion.

The first two are not identical as may be seen from a study of the *Westminster Confession of Faith*.[1] It directs ministers to declare Christ's "word and bless the elements of bread and wine . . . to take and break the bread, and they communicating also themselves to give both to the communicants, but to none who are not then present in the congregation". The next section deals with those things which are "all contrary to the nature of this sacrament and to the institution of Christ". These include private masses, the denial of the cup to the people, adoration and worshipping of the elements, and the "reserving of them for any pretended religious use". This shows clearly that the Westminster divines drew a distinction between "Giving the Communion to the Absent" and "Reservation". The latter only is condemned.

Beza, as we have seen, held that the Communion elements might be sent direct from the church to the sick person, but Calvin's view was that the Sacrament should be celebrated at the bedside of the sick. Both practices had their supporters in Scotland. It is also possible that the inclusion of the words "to none who are not then present in the congregation" in the *Confession* may be due to the fact that carrying the elements to the absent was the custom in the years preceding. There can be no doubt, however, that established Reformed practice was to celebrate Communion at the bedside of the sick. Each of the three Service-Books we are principally considering provides a Short Order for the Communion of the sick, or in special circumstances. In each it is a celebration of Communion. The Anaphora in the Scottish and English rites contains the following epiclesis:

We beseech Thee to bless and sanctify by Thy Word and Spirit these Thine own gifts of bread and wine which we set before Thee, that they may be the communion of the body and blood of Thy Son, our Saviour, Jesus Christ.

The Irish rite varies slightly, opening:

[1] *Ibid.*, 29.

We beseech Thee to bless and sanctify by Thy Word and Spirit us and these Thine own gifts of bread and wine. . . .

However, this is not the whole problem. The preface to the Scottish *Book of Common Order*, 1940, says, "Guidance is also included for the conduct of a second Table service." This opens:

In some parishes it has been customary to have a second Table at a later hour, when the communicants receive the elements already consecrated. In such cases the service may follow the preceding order until after the words of institution have been read, when the following may be used;

Beloved in the Lord; you see before you, on the Holy Table, the bread and wine which have already this day been set apart from all common uses unto this holy use and mystery; which have been sanctified by the Word of God and prayer, to be to us the Communion of the body and blood of our Saviour Jesus Christ, and the memorial of His most blessed sacrifice, once for all offered on our behalf. It is now your privilege to partake of the same Communion, that, receiving these holy gifts, you may be nourished unto everlasting life.

Then follow the Comfortable Words, an invitation to communicate, and a prayer without any reference to consecration of the elements. The service continues, as at a celebration, with the Manual Acts, *Agnus Dei*, Communion, post-communion, praise, and benediction.

Two questions may be asked here: (i) Why is it necessary to repeat the Fraction and Taking of the Cup? Surely this was done at the celebration. (ii) How is this to be reconciled with the doctrinal standards of the Church?

Customs such as the elders meeting before the Thanksgiving Service to consume what of the elements was not used, carrying out the elements in procession, and the suggestion put forward concerning the second Table in the *Book of Common Order*, 1940, raise for the writer far more problems than they answer. Dr. Moule reminds us that "an 'epiclesis', or invocation of the Holy Spirit *upon non-personal objects* is alien to the New Testament doctrine of the Holy Spirit and of persons. . . . Non-personal objects may be consecrated, that is, dedicated for a special purpose in the service of God".[1] While this is true, the writer would uphold the Reformed practice and insistence upon an "epiclesis" on the bread and wine in the Eucharist, in that it is a dedication for a special purpose in the service of God that they may be to us

[1] C. F. D. Moule, *op. cit.*, pp. 42–3.

through faith the body and blood of Christ. This being so, the purpose of the dedication is within the service, and so the possibility of Reservation does not arise.

Before turning to the question of frequency, it should perhaps be noted that Kirk-sessions during the sixteenth and early seventeenth centuries in Scotland differed considerably from those of a later period in that they seem to have been ready to have a special celebration of the Lord's Supper whenever circumstances required. For example, in Aberdeen, in 1592, certain "merchants and mariners" who were "bound to sea" were allowed to communicate on the Thursday before the regular Communion;[1] and in 1604 we find the Session in Aberdeen having a special Communion for the "merchants, skippers and mariners who were at the sail at the late ministration of the Communion; and to such other inhabitants of this burgh as were absent from the said late Communion either by reason of sickness, absence furth of the town, or otherwise".[2] In 1635 Bishop Forbes of Aberdeen, when on his death-bed, sent for the ministers of his diocese and in their company received the Communion.[3] The Ministers of Edinburgh in 1615 had the execution of the Earl of Orkney delayed until he should receive the Lord's Supper, "so he communicate upon the Lord's Day, 5th of February, and was beheaded at the Market Cross of Edinburgh on Monday 6th February".[4] In Elgin in 1622 a special Communion was held in December for "those that were sick and such others as had not communicated before".[5] Spalding records that "upon Sunday the 24th December, 1643, Communion was given to collegiars who were absent from the Communion before and to such persons as were sick and unable to come".[6] The last example shows that this practice continued to some extent in the days of the Covenant. After the Westminster Assembly the practice of admitting special Communions appears to have died out.

We have seen how Calvin's ideal was a weekly celebration of the Sacrament of the Lord's Supper as in the early church. This, indeed, was one of the points on which he quarrelled with the Genevan magis-

---

[1] J. Cooper (ed.), *Cartularium ecclesiae sancti Nicholai Aberdonensis*, 1888, p. 392.

[2] J. Stuart (ed.), *Records of the Kirk-Session, Presbytery, and Synod of Aberdeen*, 1846, i, 34.

[3] W. Anderson, *Scottish Nation*, 1863, ii, 236.

[4] D. Calderwood, *History of the Church of Scotland*, 1678, vii, 195–6.

[5] W. Crammond (ed.), *Records of Elgin*, 1897, ii, 176.

[6] J. Spalding, *Memorials of the Troubles*, 1828, ii, 301.

tracy and which led to his banishment from the city in 1538. He was prepared, however, to accept a monthly celebration and would have so arranged it that, although there was only a monthly celebration in each church, in one or other of the churches in rotation, starting with St. Pierre on the first Sunday of the month, there would be a celebration each Lord's day.[1] In Strasbourg, being in a foreign city, he adopted monthly communion. When he returned to Geneva in 1541, he knew that an attempt to secure a weekly celebration was futile owing to the prevailing popular and magisterial opinion. So he attempted to secure a monthly celebration.[2] This was disallowed by the magistracy. Thus, against his will, first monthly then quarterly Communion was forced upon Calvin.

When we turn to Scotland, the first rubric in the *Book of Common Order*, 1564, taken from the Genevan *Forme of Prayers*, 1556, says: "The day when the Lord's Supper is ministered, which is commonly once a month. . . ." On the other hand, the *First Book of Discipline* says "Four times in the year is sufficient to the administration of the Lord's Table".[3] Monthly Communion never seems to have been the practice in Scotland, this apparently being determined, not only by the shortage of Ministers, of whom there were only 289 as late as 1567, while there were 715 Readers (who could not celebrate), but by the Act of the General Assembly in 1562, which ordained, "That the Communion be administered four times in the year within the burghs, and twice in the year toward landward."[4]

So arose the Reformed custom of "infrequent communion". It must be remembered, however, that perhaps the "aura" of holy awe which surrounds Communion, with its season of special preparation, through its very infrequency has been a religious gain. On the other hand, the words of Dr. H. J. Wotherspoon require careful consideration:

Anxiety is sometimes expressed lest a frequency of celebration such as seems to have been primitive should tend to lessen its subjective impression—the awe and reverence which enhaloes it. What is the answer of experience? Looking to those areas of Christianity in which Celebration is most frequent, do we find that in those areas the sacrament is less regarded or more? less valued or waited on with less devotion or intent of heart? Something, of course, would depend on teaching: if the sacrament is regarded as an act of

[1] *CR*, x, i, 7.
[2] *CR*, x, i, 25, 213; xv, 538.
[3] *First Book of Discipline*, 11.
[4] A. Peterkin, *op. cit.*, p. 13.

pious remembering, or as only a symbolic act of fellowship, or only as an act of self-profession, one can understand that familiarity might weaken its impressiveness to the imagination or its solemnity for conscience. If it is understood as the pleading of the Sacrifice of Calvary before the Father Almighty and as the occasion of supernatural communication of his redemptive mercies, these effects do not seem to follow. It is possible that frequency of communicating disproportioned to spiritual attainment may tend to carelessness in preparation or to insensibility in reception; but attendance at Celebration, as a method of worship . . . does not seem to have that tendency.[1]

The writer would put this more strongly than "does not seem". Because it is an act of worship of God he would say "it cannot have".

Brilioth says to the Anglicans, "The problem is not solved by individual communions at an early service, followed by a high mass without communicants."[2] This is true, and the writer would say to the Reformed that neither is it solved by following a practice, such as that in St. Giles' Cathedral, Edinburgh, where after the Sunday Morning Service there is a celebration in the Moray aisle. The great service of the Lord's day must itself include communion of the people.

[1] H. J. Wotherspoon, *Religious Values in the Sacraments*, 1928, pp. 256–7.
[2] Y. Brilioth, *op. cit.*, p. 280.

VIII

ASPECTS OF THE EUCHARIST

"THE KEY to the right understanding of eucharistic doctrine," as Brilioth says, "is to be found in the liturgical services, while the formulated doctrine sometimes bears clear witness to the incapacity of merely intellectual statements to comprehend and to reproduce meanings that transcend reason."[1] Following a survey of the New Testament evidence, in which he accepts Lietzmann's[2] distinction between two types in the primitive Eucharist, one being based on Jewish family meals and the other largely Pauline, he continues,

> Our study of the New Testament evidence has already given us our starting-point, in the antitheses, evident already in the Last Supper itself, between the glad meal of fellowship and the memorial of the Lord's passion, and between the part of the communicants and that of the Lord. These antitheses may be shaped into four main elements or aspects of the eucharist: (1) *Thanksgiving*, or Eucharist; (2) *Communion-fellowship*; (3) *Commemoration*, or the historical side; (4) *Sacrifice*, including the act of Memorial, and the Church's self-oblation. To these is to be added (5) *Mystery*, which embraces and unites all the others, and bridges the gap between the one act of the Saviour and the innumerable eucharists in which that act is apprehended in the experience o faith, and its benefits appropriated.[3]

Cullmann also accepts Lietzmann's distinction, but proceeds to ask the vital question, "Is there any effective bond of unity between the two very different concepts of the Lord's Supper—between that of the primitive community and that of St. Paul?"[4] He finds the unity in the Resurrection.

The writer, therefore, would add this insight of Cullmann's to the analyses of Schweitzer,[5] Lietzmann, and Brilioth as an aspect under which to consider the Reformed rites, remembering always that these

[1] Y. Brilioth, *op. cit.*, p. 16.
[2] H. Lietzmann, *Messe and Herrenmahl*, 1926.
[3] Y. Brilioth, *op. cit.*, pp. 16–17.
[4] O. Cullmann, *op. cit.*
[5] A. Schweitzer, *Das Abendmahl im Zusammenhang mit dem Leben Jesu und der Geschichte des Urchristentums*, 1901.

aspects are a unity and are interrelated. Each involves all the others.

Brilioth's brilliant work appears to the writer to suffer from two defects: firstly, his holding that in the Reformed Church "the sacrament was treated as an appendage to the preaching-service"[1] means that he is less than fair to the Reformed rites; and, secondly, as the book was written in 1925, the most recent Reformed rite discussed is the 1924 edition of the *Euchologion*,[2] and so it requires to be brought up to date. Nevertheless, while he will outline Calvin's theology more fully than Brilioth, throughout the remainder of this chapter the writer will be much in his debt.

Let us consider the note of Thanksgiving in Calvin's theology. He writes:

> Adoration only is legitimate which stops not at the sign, but rises to Christ sitting in heaven . . . Since the Lord not only reminds us of this high gift of His goodness . . . but passes it, as it were, from hand to hand, and urges us to recognize it, He, at the same time, admonishes us not to be ungrateful for the kindness thus bestowed, but rather to proclaim it with such praise as is meet, and celebrate it with thanksgiving.[3]

When we turn to Commemoration, we find Calvin continuing the passage just quoted:

> Accordingly, when He delivered the institution of the sacrament to the apostles, He taught them to do it in remembrance of Him, which Paul interprets, "to show forth His death" (1 Cor. 11: 26). And this is that all should publicly and with one mouth confess that all our confidence of life and salvation is placed in our Lord's death, that we ourselves may glorify Him by our confession, and by our example excite others also to give Him glory. Here, again, we see what the aim of the sacrament is, namely, to keep us in remembrance of Christ's death. When we are ordered to show forth the Lord's death till He come again, all that is meant is, that we should, with confession of the mouth, proclaim what our faith has recognized in the sacrament, viz. that the death of Christ is our life.[4]

Here we have thanksgiving linked to commemoration, but he treats it as stirring us to a deeper sense of the blessings which we receive from the Lord each day, so that we offer Him the thanks and praise which are due to Him. This brings Calvin to the concept of personal self-

---

[1] Y. Brilioth, *op. cit.*, pp. 173–4.
[2] *Ibid.*, pp. 191–3.
[3] *Institutes*, iv. 17. 37.
[4] *Loc. cit.*

oblation, because it is in life that this praise and thanksgiving are to be given. Thus he says:

> It is right and fitting, that we ourselves and all our work should be sanctified and dedicated to Him that all that is in us may minister to His praise and set forth His glory. This sort of oblation has nothing to do with the propitiation of God's wrath, or with obtaining the forgiveness of our sins; it consists simply in praising and exalting God.[1]

Recognition of this aspect of the eucharistic sacrifice is "a special characteristic" of the Calvinist tradition. The remembrance of Christ's death is made by the united confession of the life and of the lips; and so this aspect is carried over from the sphere of doctrine and worship into that of service.

We find this concept also stressed in the *Westminster Confession of Faith*. The sacraments "put a visible difference between them that belong unto the Church and the rest of the world, and solemnly to engage them to the service of God in Christ, according to His word".[2]

We find the aspect of Communion-fellowship following immediately after what Calvin has to say about thanksgiving and commemoration. He says:

> The Lord intended it to be a kind of exhortation, than which no other could urge or animate us more strongly, both to purity and holiness of life, and also to charity, peace, and concord. For the Lord there communicates His body so that He may become altogether one with us, and we with Him. Moreover, since He has only one body of which He makes us all to be partakers, we must necessarily, by this participation, all become one body. This unity is represented by the bread which is exhibited in the sacrament. As it is composed of many grains, so mingled together, that one cannot be distinguished from another; so ought our minds to be so cordially united, as not to allow of any dissension or division. This I prefer giving in the words of Paul: "The cup of blessing which we bless, is it not the communion of the blood of Christ? The bread which we break, is it not the communion of the body of Christ? For we, being many, are one bread and one body, for we are all partakers of that one bread" (1 Cor. 10: 15–16). We shall have profited admirably in the sacrament, if the thought shall have been impressed and engraven on our minds, that none of our brethren is hurt, despised, rejected, injured, or in any way offended, without our, at the same time, hurting, despising, and injuring Christ; that we cannot have dissension with our brethren, without at the same time dissenting from Christ; that we cannot

---

[1] *CR*, i, 137.
[2] *WCF*, 27: 1.

love Christ without loving our brethren; that the same care we take of our own body we ought to take of that of our brethren, who are members of our body; that as no part of our body suffers pain without extending it to the other parts, so every evil which our brother suffers ought to excite our compassion. Wherefore Augustine not inappropriately often terms this sacrament "the bond of charity". What stronger stimulus could be employed to excite mutual charity, than when Christ, presenting Himself to us, not only invites us by His example to give and devote ourselves mutually to each other, but inasmuch as He makes Himself common to all, also makes us all to be one in Him.[1]

Calvin, however, in seeking to escape from the view that the Lord's Supper is a "mere commemoration" of the Lord's death fails to give adequate expression to the historical side, which is overshadowed and pushed into the background by the Communion-fellowship aspect. He so emphasizes the eternal significance thereof as the one and only means of salvation that the actual fact in history is not so prominent as it ought to be.

When we turn to Sacrifice, we find that Calvin denies that man offers anything to God by way of a "propitiatory" sacrifice in the Lord's Supper.[2] The part of man is to receive with thanksgiving all that is offered in the once-for-all sacrifice of Christ on the cross. He says:

> Christ did not offer Himself once, in the view that His sacrifice should be daily ratified by new oblations, but that by the preaching of the Gospel and the celebration of the sacred supper, the benefit of it should be communicated to us.[3]

The Lord's Supper is not a price paid to God, but a gift of God which was to be received with thanksgiving.

> In the holy Supper there is not an offering of bread and wine . . . but a mutual participation of it among the faithful (communicatio inter fideles).[4]

Again,

> The Lord has given us a table at which we may feast, not an altar on which a victim may be offered; he has not consecrated priests to sacrifice, but ministers to distribute a sacred feast.[5]

[1] Institutes, loc. cit.
[2] Ibid., iv. 18. 4.
[3] Ibid., iv. 18. 3.
[4] CR, xlix, 485–6.
[5] Institutes, iv. 18. 12.

While rejecting "propitiatory" sacrifice, Calvin accepts that there is a sacrifice offered as "a symbol and attestation of religion and divine worship", such as gifts offered "by way of thanksgiving, to testify gratitude to God for benefits received".[1] Calvin held such a sacrifice to be an "indispensable"[2] and essential part of the Lord's Supper. He says:

> The best and only worthiness which we can bring to God is to offer Him our own sinfulness, and, if I may so speak, unworthiness, that His mercy may make us worthy; to despond in ourselves, that we may be consoled in Him; to humble ourselves, that we may be justified by Him; to aspire, moreover, to the unity which He recommends in the Supper; and, as He makes us all one in Himself, to desire to have all one soul, one heart, one tongue. . . . We shall rather consider that we, who are poor, are coming to a benevolent giver, sick to a physician, sinful to the author of righteousness, in fine, dead to Him who gives life; that worthiness which is commanded by God consists especially in charity, charity, which, though imperfect, it may be sufficient to offer to God, that He may increase it, since it cannot be fully rendered.[3]

This sacrifice includes "all the offices of charity, by which, while we embrace our brethren, we honour the Lord Himself in His members; in fine all the prayers, praises, thanksgiving, and every act of worship which we return to God".[4]

In these passages Calvin emphasizes self-oblation and the offering of charity, fellowship, and love. He also names prayer as an acceptable offering.

> Though He can derive no benefit from us, yet He regards prayer as a sacrifice and so much as the chief sacrifice that it alone can supply the place of all the rest. . . . If we wish to sacrifice to God, we must call on Him and acknowledge His goodness by thanksgiving, and further, we must do good to our brethren; these are the true sacrifices.[5]

Here prayer and the daily service of God are included.

With this in mind, Calvin speaks of the "necessity that each of us should offer Christ to the Father. For although He only, and that but once, has offered Himself, still a daily offering of Him, which is effected by faith and prayers, is enjoined to us".[6] This offering is completely

[1] *Ibid.*, iv. 18. 13.
[2] *Ibid.*, iv. 18. 17.
[3] *Ibid.*, iv. 17. 42.
[4] *Ibid.*, iv. 18. 3.
[5] *CR*, lv, 194.
[6] *CR*, xxiv, 333.

different from anything accomplished through the elements of bread and wine, and is the offering "whereby alone we apply to ourselves the virtue and benefit of Christ's death".[1] For Calvin, the atoning sacrifice can only be the one sacrifice of Calvary. There can be no repetition of it. Man's sacrifice is that of self-offering and praise, thanksgiving, prayer and service.

With the note of resurrection we immediately come up against one of the major problems in Calvin's eucharistic doctrine. When discussing the person and work of Christ, he says:

> It is not by His death, but by His resurrection, that we are said to be begotten again to a living hope (1 Pet. 1: 3); because, as He, by rising again, became victorious over death, so the victory of our faith consists only in His resurrection.[2]

He continues:

> The resurrection is naturally followed by the ascension into heaven. For although Christ, by rising again, began fully to display His glory and virtue, having laid aside the abject and ignoble conditions of a mortal life, and the ignominy of the cross, yet it was only by His ascension to heaven that his reign truly commenced.[3]

Having discussed the promise of the gift of the Spirit, the resurrection appearances, and the narrative of the ascension, he concludes, quoting Augustine:

> He ascended into heaven, and is not here: for there he sits at the right hand of the Father: and yet He is here, for the presence of His Godhead was not withdrawn. Therefore, as regards His divine presence, we have Christ always; as regards His bodily presence, it was truly said to the disciples, Me ye have not always. For a few days the Church had Him bodily present. Now, she apprehends Him by faith, but sees Him not by the eye.[4]

When we examine Calvin's writings on the Lord's Supper, it has to be admitted that there are few references to the resurrection, although he does say in his *Treatise on the Lord's Supper*,

> Here then is the peculiar consolation we receive from the Supper, that it directs and conducts us to the cross of Jesus Christ and to His resurrection, in

---

[1] *Loc. cit.*
[2] *Institutes*, ii. 16. 13.
[3] *Ibid.*, ii. 16. 14.
[4] *Loc. cit.*

order to assure us that, whatever iniquity there may be in us, the Lord does not cease to regard and accept us as righteous.[1]

Of course, at the same time, it has to be remembered that the thought of Christ risen and reigning in heaven is fundamental in his theology.

While the Eucharist in the Reformed rite is always celebrated in the name and by the authority of the risen Christ, witness to the resurrection does not figure so prominently therein as it should. Indeed, the writer recently turned up a sermon he had preached in 1936, which stated:

> The *Shorter Catechism* says that the Lord's Supper is "a sacrament, wherein, by giving and receiving bread and wine, according to Christ's appointment, His death is showed forth". In this I believe the Westminster divines failed to do justice to New Testament teaching for they should have said, "His death and resurrection are shown forth."

Calvin's logic, however, leads to the crux in his doctrine. If the body of the ascended Lord has its local existence in heaven, how can he speak of a real presence in the sacrament? He attempts a solution in the *Institutes* by using the concept of the *virtus* of Christ, which is not bound by any local limitation and gives to us the benefits of His cross and passion, and, in the *Treatise*, he distinguishes between the "reality" and "substance" of the sacrament. He emphasizes that we must really partake of His body and blood, for the "reality", as God has promised, must accompany the "sign". Only so is it possible for us to possess or be possessed by the whole Christ. To partake of the spirit of Jesus is not enough: "we need to partake also of His humanity, in which he showed perfect obedience to God the Father, to make amends for our sin".[2]

Calvin so emphasizes the indivisibility of the unity of the person of Christ that he is able, in thought, without any difficulty to attribute to the human nature what belongs to the divine. He says:

> It is unlawful to dissever the flesh of Christ from His divinity. Wherever the divinity dwells, the flesh also dwells corporeally. But the deity of Christ always dwells in believers as well in life as in death; therefore so dwells the flesh. . . . I again repeat, as the divine majesty and essence of Christ fills heaven and earth, and this is extended to the flesh; therefore independently of the use of the Supper, the flesh of Christ dwells essentially in believers, because they possess the presence of His deity.[3]

[1] J. Calvin, *Treatise on the Lord's Supper*, ed. J. K. S. Reid, 1954, p. 145.
[2] *CR*, i, 507; v, 437.
[3] *CR*, ix, 509; xx, 75.

This and similar passages[1] make it easier to grasp Calvin's doctrine of the Lord's Supper, especially his emphasis on the fact that the flesh of Christ can be in heaven while exercising its virtue on earth. This miracle is the work of the Holy Spirit. He says:

> By the virtue of His Spirit and His own divine essence He not only fills heaven and earth, but also miraculously unites us with Himself in one body so that that flesh, although it remains in heaven, is our food. Thus I teach that Christ, though absent in the body, is nevertheless not only present with us by His divine energy, which is everywhere diffused, but also makes His flesh give life to us.[2]

It is noteworthy that *Confessio fidei Gallicana*, *Confessio Belgica*, *Scots Confession*, and *Westminster Confession of Faith* all agree in asserting a real presence of Christ in the Eucharist.

When we turn to the aspect of mystery, we find Calvin writing, "It is too high a mystery either for my mind to comprehend or my words to express. I rather feel than understand it (*experior magis quam intelligam*)."[3] It is the sense of holy mystery which gives depth to Calvin's presentation of Communion-fellowship, because for him the focus of the Eucharist is union with Christ, and through Him with one another.

Brilioth concludes, after examining the Reformed rites, that the elements which have been most emphasized are thanksgiving, commemoration, and above all fellowship. [4]

Let us now attempt an assessment of the Scottish, English, Irish, and Welsh rites to see how far they succeed in securing a balanced witness to these six aspects.

Thanksgiving or Eucharist

In the preparation in the Liturgy of the Word we find more of the penitential approach in the Scottish, English, and especially in the Welsh rites, although the note of thanksgiving is not completely absent. In the Irish rite, on the other hand, there is an attempt to praise God for creation, for God in Christ, and Pentecost, followed by a penitential approach. In the proclamation of the mighty acts of God in the reading and preaching of the Word the note of thanksgiving is

---

[1] *Institutes*, iv. 17. 30; iv. 17. 28; ii. 14. 2; *CR*, ix, 33, 77, 171, 195, 509; xx, 75.
[2] *CR*, ix, 76.
[3] *Institutes*, iv. 17. 32; *CR*, ix, 471.
[4] Y. Brilioth, *op. cit.*, p. 198.

certainly present. When we come to the Liturgy of the Faithful the aspect of thanksgiving in all is evident in the *Sursum corda* (not in Welsh), preface and *Sanctus*; especially is this true in the Scottish and Irish rites, which provide proper prefaces for the Christian Year. In the eucharistic prayer there is thanksgiving for the works of creation, of providence, and redemption, for the life and work of Christ, and for Pentecost. Also the post-communions sound this note. A prominent feature of the Reformed rite was psalm-singing, and this has now been extended to include hymns, and where these are linked to the Christian Year, the element of thanksgiving receives its due and proper place. This aspect is further helped by the provision of a gradual psalm in the English and Irish lectionaries, although in the latter it would almost always not be a complete psalm, but a number of verses in the metrical version. At the same time, the eucharistic note cannot ever receive full emphasis while the practice of infrequent communion continues.

Communion-fellowship

This has two sides: communion with God and with the brethren: and these become a unity in communion with Christ in the Eucharist. We cannot be members of the body of Christ without being members one of another, and thus the unity of the brethren is lifted up into the mystery of union with God. This fellowship must include the whole Church Catholic in heaven and on earth, and is unreal if it does not sanctify daily life. This note is emphasized in the common recitation of the Creed, especially in the form in the Irish rite, "We believe. . . ." The same is true in the saying together of the Lord's Prayer. All suffer, however, from a failure to extend the "saying together" to other prayers. The joining in common praise also contributes to this end. The former practice of sitting round the Table and the passing of the bread and cup from hand to hand strongly testified to the note of fellowship. The association of the worshippers with the Church Catholic is brought out in the Invitation in the Scottish and Irish rites. Fellowship with the Church Triumphant is expressed in the Thanksgiving for the Faithful Departed, especially where there is an emphasis on the eschatological note. The Eucharist must ever be seen as given to us here and now as an anticipation within history of the marriage supper of the Lamb.

Of course, once again, the note of communion-fellowship can never be completely expressed without frequent celebration, for the real expression of fellowship is the fellowship itself.

Commemoration

Turning to commemoration, we must remember that the central point which dominates all history is the death and resurrection of Christ. This, however, must be placed in its context as it does not stand in isolation. This means that the sacrament of the Lord's Supper must not take the form of simply commemorating Good Friday. It must be a commemoration of the whole redemptive purpose of God, with the centrality of the Cross placed in proper perspective. In Reformed rites, in the Liturgy of the Word the story of the passion is placed in the wider historical perspective when the Christian Year is followed, and the threefold scheme of lections is used. It is further emphasized in the Irish rite by the introduction of the Collect of the Day. It is essential therefore that the Liturgy of the Word and the Liturgy of the Faithful be seen as a unity, as is the case in all four rites we are considering. In the Liturgy of the Faithful, the note of commemoration is found in the anamnesis, which refers specifically to the main points in the story of redemption, but this is very weak in the Welsh rite. It is particularly emphasized in the Scottish and Irish rites, where the proper prefaces are of special value. The use of the Words of Institution as a scriptural warrant occurs in all four, but only in the Irish rite is the narrative of the Institution given in the Anaphora. Where the liturgical year is followed, the selection of the praise in worship helps to emphasize the note of commemoration and also to keep it in perspective. One real weakness here in all four rites is a failure to represent the story of redemption as continued in the life of the Church. The observance of All Saints and Reformation Sunday (in the Irish rite) helps here. The only place in which this would appear to receive due recognition is in the thanksgivings for the faithful and a proper use of Church history in preaching. The provision of "Themes" in the Irish Lectionary, also, contributes to this end.

Sacrifice

When discussing the eucharistic Sacrifice, Brilioth says:

In the deepest sense, Christianity acknowledges one sacrifice only, the self-oblation of God Himself in Christ. In Christian worship, therefore, there can be no act of sacrifice or oblation which is not subordinated to the one supreme sacrifice. . . . The Christian has in truth but one gift which he can give to God, namely himself; and the eucharist could not be the central act of Christian worship if it did not include and express this idea. . . . The

Eucharist is the church's supreme act of prayer, the pleading of the one sacrifice.[1]

The emphasis on the memorial aspect of the once-for-all sacrifice of Christ is clearly set out in the Manual Acts in the Scottish, English and Irish rites. It is also evident in the Anaphora in all four, and in the Offertory prayers in the Scottish and English rites.

The anamnesis in the Scottish and English rites says:

Wherefore, having in remembrance the work and passion of our Saviour Christ, and pleading His eternal sacrifice, we Thy servants do set forth this memorial. . . .

The Irish rite has:

Wherefore, having in remembrance the sufferings and death of our Lord Jesus Christ, His glorious resurrection and ascension, we Thy servants do set forth this memorial. . . .

While the Irish rite is an improvement in that it adds a reference to the resurrection and ascension, it is very much weaker because of the omission of "pleading His eternal sacrifice".[2] The emphasis here is not simply upon "the oblation once offered" on the cross, though that is included, but specifically upon the eternal significance of our Lord's sacrifice. Christ's atoning death and resurrection happened once for all in time, but they belong to eternity. So also the Eucharist is of eternity; and when we plead His eternal sacrifice we desire Him to unite our offering and prayers with His, which are eternal, and this memorial in time and space is a part of that eternal memorial. His sacrifice is not repeatable, but it is continually renewed; the remembering is not mere commemoration, but a real uniting, possible by grace and through faith. This is not mere intellectual assent, but a committal of the whole person to Him, and that not simply as an individual, but also corporately within the Church.

As Brilioth points out, we are "pleading the one sacrifice of Christ" every time we pray "through Jesus Christ our Lord".[3]

The note of self-oblation in the Welsh rite is placed in the post-communion, but in the other three receives its proper place in the Anaphora. It is:

Here we offer and present unto Thee ourselves, our souls and bodies, to be a

[1] *Ibid.*, pp. 282-3.
[2] It was in the original draft, but later had to be omitted.
[3] *Loc. cit.*

reasonable, holy and living sacrifice; and we beseech Thee mercifully to accept this our sacrifice of praise and thanksgiving, as, in fellowship with all the faithful in heaven and on earth, we pray Thee to fulfil in us, and in all men, the purpose of Thy redeeming love. . . .

Resurrection

Turning to the aspect of resurrection, we find that these rites, as is common in Western Christianity, place the principal emphasis on the death and sacrifice of Christ. It has to be admitted that the rite is celebrated "in the name of" the risen Lord, and also that the only true celebrant is Jesus Christ Himself, present in the midst of His people. Also, every minister in the Reformed Church would say with St. Paul, "If Christ be not risen then is our preaching a vain thing."[1] We find witness to this note in the Creed and in the prayer of consecration, the Irish rite adding a reference to it, as we have seen, in the anamnesis. On the other hand, apart from what reference there may be thereto in the hymns, only the Irish rite links the resurrection to the Eucharist by adding after the narrative of the Institution in the Anaphora, "We bless thee . . . that after He was risen He was known to His disciples in the breaking of bread."

The writer wonders if it would be fair to ask whether or not it is a failure to grasp the fullness of the relationship of the Eucharist and the resurrection which has prevented the Reformed Churches from recovering the practice of frequent communion.

Mystery

The element of mystery may be seen, although not so prominently as formerly, in the stress laid on preparation for communion, all four rites providing a service for this purpose. In the Scottish, English, and Irish rites the Eucharist is referred to twice as a mystery. In the confession of sin in the preparation in the Liturgy of the Word, God is addressed as: Our Father, "who admittest Thy people into such wonderful communion that, partaking by a divine mystery of the body and blood of Thy dear Son, they should dwell in Him, and He in them. . . ."

Again, in the Liturgy of the Faithful, at the Taking to set apart the elements "I (Irish, "We") take these elements of bread and wine to be set apart from all common uses to this holy use and mystery".

The note of mystery appears in three chief ways: (i) the personal

[1] I Cor. 15: 14.

presence of the Lord "in the midst" as the true celebrant; (ii) the presence of the Lord in the sacrament, the sacred elements being, according to His own words, His body and blood, the means of His presence and of His self-communication; and (iii) the presence of Christ in His mystical body, whereby those who are united to Christ are united also to one another and share in the communion of saints.[1] These are complementary, and are all essential notes of the Eucharist.

The first is expressed in the Scottish rite by the words, "Let us worship God." The Irish rite having proclaimed God as Creator, Redeemer and immanent, says, "Let us worship and praise God." From the very first moment of worship the people see themselves as in the very presence of God. The English and Welsh rites do not, on the other hand, state this so clearly, although it is also true in doctrine.

The second type of mystery has been illustrated above from the prayer for forgiveness, but it is also evident from the epiclesis in the Scottish, English and Irish rites. It is substantially the same in all three, the text quoted being the Irish:

> We most humbly beseech Thee through the Holy Spirit to sanctify both us and these Thine own gifts of bread and wine which we set before Thee, that the bread which we break may be the communion of the body of Christ, and the cup of blessing which we bless the communion of the blood of Christ: that we, receiving them, may by faith be made partakers of His Body and Blood. . . .

It is also witnessed to in the words of distribution:

> Take, eat, this is the body of Christ. . . . This cup is the new covenant in the blood of Christ. . . .

It also appears in the Offertory prayers in the Scottish and English rites.

The third type of mystery appears in the prayers of supplication, in the intercessions for the Church, and in the thanksgivings for the Faithful Departed, but perhaps finds fullest expression in the self-oblation, quoted above, where the self-offering is "in fellowship with all the faithful in heaven and on earth", in the name of Christ.

In conclusion, we have seen how the Eucharist for Calvin involves brotherly fellowship, mutual love, holiness of character and conduct. The worship of the Church is the stimulus to Christian life in the world. The service of God (liturgy) leads inevitably to the service of

---

[1] Y. Brilioth, *op. cit.*, p. 286.

men for the glory of God. Worship is the basis for and motivating force to Christian citizenship and service that "the kingdoms of this world may become the kingdom of our God and of His Christ". In others words, in worship, especially in the Eucharist, we praise God, share in the common life of the body of Christ, are built up in Christian faith and love, to share in the witness and service of Christ and His Church to the world. While undoubtedly this concept underlies all these rites it receives its fullest expression in the Irish with the addition before the benediction of the dismissal, "Go forth in the peace of Christ to serve Him in the world."

IX

THE BAPTISMAL RITE

THE CONCEPT of God as a Covenant God and of the Church consisting "of all those throughout the world that profess the true religion together with their children"[1] means that baptism must be seen as an integral act of worship within the Reformed Church, and that rites must be provided for the baptism of the infant children of believers, for to be a Presbyterian it is essential to be a "Paedo-baptist". It is necessary, therefore, that we should review the rites in the Reformed liturgies.

A survey of the baptismal rites in the Western Church at the eve of the Reformation shows that an amazing number of ceremonies had been added to the practice of the early Church, as recorded in the *Didache*,[2] Justin Martyr,[3] and Hippolytus' *Apostolic Tradition*.[4] Dr. G. W. Bromiley says:

> It was always admitted, of course, that these ceremonies were not essential to the sacrament, so that the omission of them in emergency cases did not in any way affect its validity or efficacy. But where the ceremonies could be had, the Schoolmen defended them on the ground that they belonged to the solemnity of the occasion, that they had value for purposes of edification and that in some cases they helped to remove obstacles to grace (e.g. exorcism and spittle), or contributed to the virtue and power of the sacrament (e.g. oil).[5]

Against this, the Council of Trent anathematized those who said that "the received and approved rites of the catholic church may be contemned . . . or omitted".[6]

In the early Church, baptism was celebrated within the eucharistic context,[7] the order of worship being:

[1] *WCF*, 25: 2.
[2] *Didache*, 7.
[3] Justin, *op. cit.*, i, 61, 65.
[4] Hippolytus, *op. cit.*, 16–23.
[5] G. W. Bromiley, *Baptism and the Anglican Reformers*, 1953, p. 148.
[6] H. Denzinger, *Enchiridion*, 1932, 856.
[7] Hippolytus, *op. cit.*, 23.

Liturgy of the Word
Baptism
Confirmation
Liturgy of the Faithful.

Later this ceased to be the case. Also, from the thirteenth century the service of Confirmation became permanently separated from Baptism by a period of seven to fourteen years, because it was only rarely that a bishop was available to administer the rite.[1]

Calvin in his letter of farewell to the ministers, in 1564, says, "I was constrained also to make the Baptismal Order, being in Strasbourg, and because they brought to me children of anabaptists from five or six leagues around to baptize them. This form was plain, but I don't advise you to change it. . . ."[2] This has led Dr. W. D. Maxwell, and others, to say, "Calvin himself claimed authorship for the Baptismal Service in his *La Forme*. . . . An examination of the other Reformed orders, German and French, bears out the truth of Calvin's statement, for there is little or no connexion between Calvin's order and these either in content or general order."[3]

The writer, having examined the texts personally, cannot agree with this statement, and accepts the position of Dr. W. D. Bailie,[4] Dr. F. O. Reed,[5] and Dr. G. J. van de Poll[6] that Calvin was indebted to Bucer and especially to Farel, who had based his Baptismal Order on those in existence in Strasbourg from 1525-33. Having set out the structure and analysed the text of Farel's *La Manière* and Calvin's Strasbourg *La Forme*, Dr. Bailie writes:

> The evidence presented in the above table may be summarised as follows: (1) The Scripture sentence (Ps. cxxiv, 8) is identical in both rites. (2) The initial question to the sureties concerning their desire to have the child baptised has a similarity in wording. (3) There are phrases in the Pre-baptismal prayer which are common to both rites. (4) The words of introduction to the reading of the Gospel (St. Matt. xix, 13-15) are closely related, and the texts of the Gospel passage, while not exactly identical, are very similar. (5) A considerable portion of the Promise or Exhortation to the sureties to instruct the child in the Christian faith is identical. (6) The rubrics directing

[1] *Encyclopaedia of Religion and Ethics*, art. Baptism.
[2] *CR*, ix, 894.
[3] *JKGSB*, p. 48.
[4] W. D. Bailie, *The Rites of Baptism and Confirmation*, (MS., 1959).
[5] F. O. Reed, *Worship in 16th century Calvinism*, (MS., 1933).
[6] G. J. van de Poll, *Martin Bucer's Liturgical Ideas*, 1954.

the Minister to baptise the child have some similarity in wording. (7) The Prayer of blessing (Post-baptismal prayer) is identical in both rites.[1]

Calvin's Strasbourg rite was further simplified for use in Geneva, and was the determining influence in the Genevan *Forme of Prayers*, 1556, and the Scottish *Book of Common Order*, 1564. The following is the structural outline of Calvin's Strasbourg rite:

1. Scripture Sentence: Our help is in the name of the Lord. . . .
2. Question: Do you present this child to be baptized, earnestly desiring that he may be ingrafted in the mystical body of Christ?
3. Long exhortation and exposition
4. Prayer for grace and reception of child into the Kingdom of Christ
5. Lord's Prayer
6. Question: Do you wish this child baptized. . . ?
7. Apostles' Creed
8. Short exhortation to instruct child
9. Baptism
10. Declaration that the child is a member of Christ

The *Forme of Prayers*, 1556, alters the order of this considerably, including 2, 3, 7, 4, 5, 9, and a concluding thanksgiving and prayer for the blessing of the Holy Spirit in that sequence. The *Book of Common Order*, 1564, follows the *Forme of Prayers*.

Certain features of the Reformed rites require notice. Whereas other traditions superimpose a Baptismal Order upon the existing mediaeval rite, which was designed in the first place for the baptism of adult believers, the Reformed rites are entirely new Orders from which all non-scriptural elements are omitted, and which are also designed to be relevant to the baptism of infants. Exorcisms and renunciations are laid aside as being inappropriate to the baptism of children of Christian parents.[2] No vicarious profession of faith is required of the father or godfather, the children being admitted to baptism on the grounds of the Covenant of grace. The Creed is repeated by the parents or sponsors as the faith which they themselves believe as members of the Church of Christ and into which they wish the child baptized, they being required to take a vow to bring up the child therein. While there is no objection to godparents, the chief sponsor is, generally speaking, the father of the child. Baptism is normally by affusion. In the early

---

[1] W. D. Bailie, *op. cit.*, chap. ii, p. 22.
[2] *New Schaff-Herzog Encyclopedia*, i, 444.

Reformed rites no prayer for the sanctification of the water to its holy use is given. The reason was either that it was not included in the mediaeval rite, being a separate act of worship, or that the statement of intention of baptism was held to be sufficient.

It should perhaps be pointed out that baptism was always placed in the setting of the worship of the people of God. The rite followed the reading and preaching of the Word, and was to be administered only "in the face of the congregation".

The *Book of Common Order*, 1564, was replaced by the *Westminster Directory* in 1645. Its Order for Baptism is:

> Exhortation
> Prayer, including the blessing of the water
> Enquiry as to name
> Baptism
> Prayer of thanksgiving and for the blessing
>   of the Holy Spirit

Commenting on the *Directory* Sprott says, it

does not prescribe any profession of faith to be exacted of sponsors. In Scotland they had always been made to rehearse the Creed, as required by the Book of Common Order; and the Scottish Commissioners at Westminster earnestly contended for the general adoption of this practice. Failing in this, they urged that questions equivalent should be asked, and assented to. . . . These interrogations have disappeared from the Directory, and it has been supposed that they were struck out by the House of Commons. In Scotland the old custom lingered on for a time.[1]

The service for Baptism in the *Directory* remained the legal standard of the Church, but much laxity arose in practice in Scotland as, indeed, elsewhere.

The *Euchologion* of the Church Service Society, which did so much to uplift Scottish worship, contained a service for the Baptism of infants, which was based on ancient sources as well as the liturgies of the Reformation. It came into widespread use, and all modern Reformed rites are derived from it.

Before considering these, a few remarks must be made about emergency baptism and the baptismal rites for adults. Private baptism was not permitted in any circumstances in the early days of the Scottish reformation. The Perth Articles of 1618 allowed it, but only "for a great and necessary cause". This was annulled by the Glasgow Assembly

---

[1] G. W. Sprott, *Worship and Offices of the Church of Scotland*, 1882, pp. 65–6.

of 1638. The *Westminster Directory*, 1645, forbids baptism "in any case" by a "private person", and expressly states that it is not to be administered "in private places, or privately, but in the place of public worship, and in the face of the congregation". However, during the late eighteenth century private baptism became common. Today the recovery of baptism within the setting of the worshipping congregation is almost complete, even in Ireland.

While modern Service-Books make no special provision for private baptism, the necessity for the celebration of the rite privately in special circumstances, such as sickness, is admitted.[1] In practice the form for public baptism, abbreviated at the discretion of the minister, is used on such occasions. It, of course, must be with water in the Triune name.[2]

So far as baptism of adult believers is concerned, there is no provision made for such services in the early Reformed liturgies or in the *Westminster Directory*. The Dutch Church, as it was the first to undertake missionary work overseas, was the first to provide such a form. This was in 1604, and it remains the basis of modern Reformed rites. Provision for such a service was made in the third edition of the *Euchologion*, 1874, opening with the Scriptural sentence, "Our help is in the name of the Lord . . ." after which the Minister asks the person to be baptized: "Do you present yourself for Holy Baptism, desiring to be ingrafted into the body of Christ?" The modern Scottish, English, and Irish rites have been deeply influenced by the *Euchologion*.

The Scottish Service-Book entitles the Baptismal rites, "Order for the Administration of the Sacrament of Baptism to Infants" and "Order for the Administration of the Sacrament of Baptism to Adults". The English rite divides "The Order for the Administration of the Sacrament of Baptism" into "The Baptism of Infants" and "The Baptism of Adults". The Irish rite, recognizing that the Reformed Church does not baptize adults and infants, more correctly entitles the services "The Baptism of Believers" and "The Baptism of the Children of Believers".

Let us discuss first the rite for the baptism of the infant children of believers. The rites we shall consider as setting forth the ideal for England and Ireland are those in the *Presbyterian Service Book* and the *Book of Public Worship* respectively, but for Scotland, instead of using the Order in the *Book of Common Order*, 1940, we shall take the "Order for the Administration of Holy Baptism", published in 1963. The

[1] *The Book of Common Order*, 1928; *A New Directory for the Public Worship of God*, 1898.

[2] WCF, 28: 2.

baptismal service is a unity, but for the sake of analysis it may be divided into sections. Let us look first at the section prior to the taking of vows.

The Scottish and English rites are structurally similar here and may be dealt with together. After the singing of a baptismal hymn, the minister says, "Our help is in the name of the Lord, who made heaven and earth," the English adding, "And who redeems us in Jesus Christ His Son, our Saviour."

The English form continues with the minister saying:

All born into this world are subject to sin and death, but through His grace God has given us in Jesus Christ His Son our Lord, who died and rose again for our salvation, pardon for our sins and eternal life. Being born again of the Holy Spirit, we are brought into a new relationship with God.

Baptism is the visible sign of this new relationship and new birth. Just as water washes stains from the body, so in this Sacrament the Holy Spirit purifies our souls from sin, and enables us to be reborn into eternal life.

There is nothing parallel to this in the Scottish rite.

In both now comes St. Matthew 28: 18–20, the English rite, as in the *Book of Common Order*, 1940, describing this as "the institution of the Holy Sacrament of Baptism", whereas the Scottish simply says, "Hear the words of our Lord Jesus Christ who . . . gave commandment to His disciples, saying. . . ."

The Scottish rite continues:

Holy Baptism is administered in obedience to our Lord Jesus Christ, who in the days of His flesh took upon Himself the sins of the whole world, and submitted to the Baptism of John in the river Jordan. At His Baptism, He was anointed by the Holy Spirit for His saving work, which He triumphantly accomplished in His Death, Resurrection and Ascension.

On the Day of Pentecost, as He had promised, the church was baptized with the Holy Spirit, and the Apostle Peter called upon the people, saying: "Repent, and be baptized. . . ."

There is no parallel to this in the English service.

Both continue with paragraphs setting forth baptism as a sign and seal of ingrafting into Christ . . . of forgiveness and cleansing . . . that thereby we are admitted into membership of the Church . . . that the children of believers are within this covenant and promise, leading up to St. Mark 10: 13–16, "They brought young children to Jesus. . . ." The Scottish rite ends with the Marcan passage, but the English adds:

Here our Lord makes known His desire to receive little children, and also the necessity for the child's virtues of simplicity, candour, and trust, in those who seek Christ's Kingdom.

The wording of the section outlined above in the English rite is almost identical with the *Book of Common Order*, 1940. The new Scottish Order is much more brief and direct.

The Irish rite differs considerably in this section. It opens with the rubric:

Following the Thanksgiving and Dedication of ourselves and our offerings, the child shall be brought to the font by the parents and/or sponsors during the singing of a baptismal hymn, after which the minister shall say: "Hear the Word of God. . . ."

Here, as in the Scottish rite, baptism is to be administered at Divine Service after sermon.

Then are given several scriptural passages: God's covenant with Abraham, the baptism of Jesus, Peter's proclamation on the day of Pentecost, St. Mark 10: 13–16 and St. Matthew 28: 18–20.

This is followed by a Statement of Intention:

The Covenant of God is held forth to believers and their children.

The Sacrament of Baptism through the Christian centuries has been accepted as the seal of God upon the children, as the appointed means of admission to the Church of Christ, and as a solemn act whereby their participation in God's covenant of forgiveness and redemption in Christ is proclaimed.

In accordance with God's purpose revealed in His Covenant, the mind and spirit of Christ, and the practice of the Church of Christ the child of Mr. and Mrs. N. . . . is now presented for baptism.

This may be open to the criticism that it is not a full enough statement of the meaning of baptism, but does one really need long expositions in the actual service where there has been proper instruction? One of the instructions given in the Irish rite is, "Parents ought to receive instruction in the meaning of Baptism before the admission of their children to this Sacrament." While not specifically mentioned in the Scottish and English books, it is the common practice that this should be done.

Let us now turn to the section of the service dealing with the vows. To this much thought has been given in recent years as to how to make the vows more meaningful to parents and sponsors. The English rite says:

In presenting this child for Baptism, do you confess your faith in God as your heavenly Father, in Jesus Christ as your Saviour and Lord, and in the Holy Spirit as your Sanctifier?

Alternatively the Apostles' Creed may be used.

Do you promise, in dependence on Divine grace, to teach him the truths and duties of the Christian faith; and by prayer, precept and example, to bring him up in the knowledge and love of the Lord, and in the ways of the Church of God?

If there are sponsors present the Minister says to them:

Do you confess anew your faith in God your Father, in Jesus Christ your Lord and Saviour, and in the Holy Spirit your Sanctifier, and do you undertake, should need arise, to do all you can for this child's instruction and godly upbringing?

Then the Minister says:

The Lord bless you and your child(ren), and give you grace faithfully to perform these promises.

These are substantially the questions which have been addressed to parents and sponsors within Presbyterianism for the best part of a century.

In the Scottish rite there has been a new approach in that Calvin's first question has been restored, as in the first edition of the *Euchologion* (it is omitted from the second onwards), and a common confession of faith is required from the whole congregation during the celebration. It is:

Do you present this child to be baptized, earnestly desiring that he may be ingrafted into the mystical body of Jesus Christ?

Do you believe in one God, Father, Son, and Holy Spirit; and do you confess Jesus Christ as your Saviour and Lord?

Do you promise, God being your helper, to teach this child the truths and duties of the Christian faith; and by prayer, precept, and example, to bring him up in the nurture and admonition of the Lord, and in the ways of the Church of God?

Then the Minister shall say:

The Lord preserve you and the child and enable you to fulfil these promises.

Then addressing the congregation, he shall say:

Dearly beloved, These vows have been made in the presence of God and of you, His people. They can be fulfilled only within the fellowship and discipline of the Church. Therefore let all stand and confess the faith.

Then is said the Apostles' Creed.

While the reintroduction of Calvin's first question is to be commended, yet are not the questions still too traditional? Also, should the second question not include some reference to the Holy Spirit as Sanctifier?

In the Irish rite an attempt is made to involve the congregation in responsibility for the future of the child, and the question to the parents, taken from the *Book of Common Worship* of the Church of South India, is an attempt to state it in more practical language. It is:

In presenting this child for Baptism do you profess your faith in God as your Creator and Father, in Jesus Christ as your Lord and Saviour, and in the Holy Spirit as your Sanctifier and Guide?

Will you, by God's help, provide a Christian home, and bring up this child in the worship and teaching of the Church, so that your child may come to know Jesus Christ as Lord and Saviour?

To the congregation:

Do you, who now in Christ's name receive this child into the fellowship of the Church, promise, by God's help, so to order your congregational life and witness that he may grow up in the knowledge and love of God and be continually surrounded by Christian example and influence?

The Minister shall say:

The Lord give you grace faithfully to fulfil these promises.

Here the reference to the "Christian home" in the question to the parents is to be commended, and also the involvement of the congregation in the necessity for a Christian ordering of its life and witness.

In all rites now comes the baptismal prayer. In the Scottish rite it opens with the *Sursum corda*, which was also in the original Irish draft, but had to be omitted. Then comes an ascription to the Trinity, followed by:

We beseech Thee, O Lord our God, to send forth Thy Holy Spirit to sanctify us all and to bless this water to the mystical washing away of sin, that this child, being born anew of water and the Holy Spirit, may receive the fullness of Thy Grace, and ever be found in the number of Thine elect: Grant that his name may be written in the Lamb's Book of Life, and that, buried with Christ in Baptism, he may rise with Christ into newness of life, and be numbered with Thy saints in glory everlasting; through the same Jesus Christ our Lord.

Apart from the fact that it too contains an epiclesis, the English prayer is very different. It is:

Most merciful and loving Father, we thank Thee for the Church of Thy Son our Saviour, the ministry of Thy Word, and the Sacraments of grace.

Especially do we praise Thee now for the institution of this Sacrament of Holy Baptism, wherein Thou dost give such gracious promises for our children and dost seal them in Christ for Thine own. Do Thou sanctify this element of water for the spiritual use to which Thou hast ordained it, and grant that this child now to be baptized therewith may be born again of water and the Holy Spirit and ever remain in the number of Thy faithful children, through Jesus Christ our Lord.

These two rites place the prayers for the home and the assembled congregation in the post-baptismal prayers. The Irish rite, on the other hand, places all within the baptismal prayer. It opens with thanksgiving to God for His work of creation, especially the creation of man "in Thine own image", and for His providence and mercy, a thanksgiving for Christ and redemption in Him, an epiclesis for "us and this water" as in the *Book of Common Order*, 1940, a prayer for the child, for his home and parents, followed by a self-oblation, beseeching God to "Quicken us anew by the power of Thy Holy Spirit, that we may walk in charity, humility, and godliness, as those who have been baptized by the same Spirit into one body. . . ."

Baptism "in the name of the Father, and of the Son, and of the Holy Spirit", follows in all three rites. Then the minister says, "The blessing of God Almighty, Father, Son, and Holy Spirit, be upon thee, and abide in thee for ever." This is the Irish form; the Scottish and English rites have "descend upon thee, and dwell in thine heart forever".

In the Scottish and English rites the Aaronic Blessing may then be sung, but in the Irish rite this is not sung until after the Declaration. The latter is the more correct for the Declaration is part of the actual baptism. The Scottish rite of Confirmation, as we shall see, places it after the Declaration. In the Irish rite the Declaration is:

This child is now received, according to Christ's commandment, into the membership of the holy Catholic Church, and engaged to be the Lord's.

In passing, it is of interest to note that it is in connexion with the Declaration that American Presbyterianism has attempted to witness to the involvement of the congregation. The Declaration in the *Book of Common Worship*, 1946, of the Presbyterian Church in the United States of America is:

This child is now received into Christ's Church: And you the people of this congregation in receiving this Child promise with God's help to be his sponsor to the end that he may confess Christ as his Lord and Saviour and come at last to His eternal kingdom. Jesus said, Whoso shall receive one such little child in My name receiveth Me.

The opinion of the writer, however, is that this is better witnessed to in connexion with the vows before baptism.

The Irish rite ends with the Aaronic blessing, and the Apostolic benediction. The Scottish and English rites place the Aaronic blessing before the Declaration, which is followed by prayers for the child, for his home, and for ourselves, the Lord's Prayer, a hymn, and benediction. In the Scottish rite, St. Matthew 18: 5, 6, 10 may be read between the Declaration and the prayers.

The rites for the baptism of believers call for only a few comments as much of what has already been said applies to them, but there are one or two significant points.

The Scottish and English rites open with the same Scriptural Sentences as for infants and retain most of the exposition. The principal changes are that both omit the reference to St. Mark 10: 13–16 and the English rite adds a reference to Acts 2: 38–9. The exposition in the *Book of Common Order*, 1940, which that in the English rite substantially resembles, ends thus:

> This call to repentance and faith in Jesus Christ, and to confession thereof in this Sacrament, is addressed to you. Be assured that as you truly profess your faith and are baptized into His name, this Sacrament shall be to you the sign and seal of the washing away of your sins, of your ingrafting into Christ, of your regeneration by the Holy Spirit, and of your engagement to be the Lord's.

The Irish rite opens with the same rubric as in the service for the baptism of the children of believers, and the readings are Peter's sermon at Pentecost, the baptism of Jesus, and St. Matthew 28: 18–20. Then comes the Statement of Intention:

> Baptism is a Sacrament, ordained by Jesus Christ, to be to us a sign and seal of our ingrafting into Him; of remission of sins, and regeneration by His Spirit; of reception into the Church of God, and resurrection unto eternal life; and of our response unto God, through Jesus Christ, to walk in newness of life.
>
> In accordance with God's purpose revealed in His Covenant, N. . . . doth now present himself for baptism on profession of faith.

The vows in the Scottish and English rites are identical. Firstly, a confession of the Apostles' Creed in the declaratory form, and then:

> Do you repent of your sins with a humble and contrite heart, and put your trust in the mercy of God which is in Christ Jesus?

Do you promise to make diligent use of the means of grace, and to be a faithful member of the Church of God?

The Irish rite, too, requires confession of the Apostles' Creed, but here it is put in question form as in Hippolytus' *Apostolic Tradition*.[1] This is followed by the third question as in the Scottish and English rites. Then comes a further question, once again, as in the rite for infants, addressed to the congregation:

> Do you, who now in Christ's name receive this fellow-believer into the fellowship of the Church, promise, by God's help, so to order your congregational life and witness that he may be enabled to grow in grace in the worship and service of Jesus Christ?

When we turn to the rest of the rite the comments above concerning the Order for the baptism of the children of believers are relevant here, but two points require special comment. Firstly, in the Irish rite, the prayer, "Strengthen and confirm him, we beseech thee, through the Holy Spirit; and daily increase in him the manifold gifts of Thy grace . . ." is included in the baptismal prayer; and after baptism the newly-baptized is given the right hand of fellowship. In other words a later Confirmation Service is not required.

Secondly, appended to the Scottish rite is a note:

> Persons baptized when adults should be informed that in the Service of Confirmation of Baptized persons and Admission to the Lord's Supper there are expressions which do not apply to them.

Here is a change in Scottish practice. In the *Euchologion*, following the baptism with water in the triune name, the Minister blesses the person baptized, "with imposition of hands", saying:

> The very God of peace sanctify you wholly; and I pray God your whole spirit, and soul, and body, be preserved blameless unto the coming of the Lord Jesus Christ.

Then comes the Declaration:

> This person is now received by Christ's appointment into His Church, to be a partaker of the Lord's Supper, and of all the privileges of the new covenant, and is engaged to confess the faith of Christ crucified, and to continue Christ's faithful soldier and servant unto his life's end.

This was true of all later editions of the *Euchologion*, and is that

[1] Hippolytus, *op. cit.*, 21.

adopted in the *New Directory for the Public Worship of God*, 1898, of the Free Church, in *Presbyterian Forms of Service*, 1899, of the United Presbyterian Church, and in the *Book of Common Order*, 1964, of the Presbyterian Church of Canada. With a different approach it is also the standpoint of the *Book of Common Order*, 1932, of the United Church of Canada, and the *Book of Common Worship*, 1946, of the Presbyterian Church in the United States of America. It is also the intention, although there is no rubric directing the laying on of hands, because this was objected to, of the *Book of Public Worship*, 1965, of the Presbyterian Church in Ireland, which states, "This Sacrament admits to membership of the Church and to the Table of the Lord." The writer feels that if the laying on of hands at the Blessing after the baptism were restored, the standpoint of the *Euchologion* is to be preferred to that of the *Book of Common Order*, 1940, and would witness to a more correct doctrine of baptism-confirmation as one rite as in the early Church.

X

THEOLOGY IN THE BAPTISMAL RITE

WE SAW above that Christian doctrines may be divided into Catholic, Evangelical, and Particular. When baptism is celebrated in the setting of the worshipping community what was said concerning the first two is relevant, and so there is no need for detail here. At the same time, with regard to the first we should perhaps quote Professor T. F. Torrance:

> We are not baptized into the name of Christ only, but also into the name of the Father and of the Holy Spirit. This is very important, for it indicates that the meaning of Baptism cannot be determined exclusively with reference to Christ. Baptism is concerned with the eternal love of the Father and with His gracious decision to reconcile us in His Son, and to adopt us as His children; and it is equally concerned with the sanctifying and renewing work of the Creator Spirit. Thus Baptism in the name of the Father speaks of the pre-venient love of God, and tells us that long before we learned to love and believe in Him He loved us and chose us to be His own; and Baptism in the name of the Holy Spirit speaks of the supernatural presence and work of God, telling us that our coming to love Him and our learning to believe in Him are the creative work of the Holy Spirit within us. It is only within that context of Baptism in the name of the Father and of the Holy Spirit that we can speak rightly of Baptism in the name of Christ. On the other hand, because the eternal love of God was incarnated in Jesus Christ, and because the Father sends us His Holy Spirit in the name of Christ, it remains true that the significance of Baptism is essentially Christocentric.[1]

One further point requires to be made. Professor Torrance says:

> The New Testament writers employ an unusual word for Baptism and attach to it a distinctive meaning. This is the term *baptisma* which is to be interpreted in much the same way as another important New Testament term, *kerygma*. *Kerygma* refers to the proclamation of the Gospel, and yet not so much to the proclamation itself as to what is proclaimed, namely, Jesus Christ. . . . Similarly in regard to Baptism, the New Testament is not interested so much in the outward rite as in what stands behind the rite; not so much in the subjective experience of the baptized as in the death and resurrection of Christ. . . . This indicates that Baptism is to be interpreted not

[1] T. F. Torrance, *op. cit.*, ii, 128.

in relation to what we do but in relation to what God in Christ has done and will do for us; its meaning does not lie in the rite itself and its performance, or in the attitude of the baptized and his confession of faith, important though they are. It lies beyond—in Christ.[1]

When Professor James Barr says that *kerygma* is no analogy for *baptisma*,[2] one may agree with him linguistically, but it has to be remembered that *baptisma* cannot be treated in abstraction. It is *baptisma* of the *kerygma*. Baptism is a sacrament of the Gospel. So even if we agree with Barr linguistically, Torrance's statement is nevertheless theologically true.

With regard to Evangelical doctrines, the headship of Christ is seen in that what is done is done "in Christ's name", prayer is made to God "through Him", and the Declaration states that what is done is "according to Christ's commandment". The primacy of scriptural authority is evident in the use of Scripture readings as the authority for the action of the Church. The priesthood of believers is evident in the admission to membership in the Church of Christ.

In reference to particular doctrines, to understand the significance and meaning of baptism within the Reformed rites, let us attempt first to outline Calvin's teaching, and then proceed to an assessment of the Scottish, English-Welsh (which may be treated as one), and Irish Orders.

Calvin's doctrine of baptism is possibly best summarized as "the sign of ingrafting into Christ". In baptism the baptized person, as a member of Christ, is placed within a new sphere of common life which the members of Christ share with their exalted Head. The baptism of an individual is the sharing of one common baptism, which the whole Church shares in common with Christ, Himself baptized in Jordan. It is a common baptism in which the whole Church is made one body in union with Christ. " 'One baptism' means," says Calvin, "that one baptism is common to all; so that by means of it we begin to form one body and soul."[3] Jesus, he says, "consecrated and sanctified baptism in His own body that He might have it in common with us as the foremost bond of union and fellowship which He deigned to form with us; and hence Paul proves us to be sons of God from the fact that we have put on Christ in baptism (Gal. 3: 27)".[4] Again he says, "He received

---

[1] *Ibid.*, ii, 127.
[2] J. Barr, *The Semantics of Biblical Language*, 1961, pp. 140–4.
[3] *CR*, li, 191.
[4] *Institutes*, iv. 15. 6.

baptism with us, in order to assure believers that they are ingrafted into His body, and that they are buried with Him in baptism, that they may rise to newness of life (Rom. 6: 4). . . . The general reason why Christ received baptism was that He might render full obedience to the Father; and the special reason was that He might consecrate baptism in His own body, that we might have it in common with Him."[1] The Church through her baptism becomes the redeemed body that shares not only a great experience of redemption, as did Israel at the Red Sea, but the one life of the Redeemer. Thus baptism is rightly made the sign of initiation by which a person is received into the Church visible. "As baptism," he says, "is a solemn recognition by which God introduces His children into the possession of life, a true and effectual sealing of the promise, a pledge of sacred union with Christ, it is justly said to be the entrance and reception into the Church."[2]

He also sees baptism as a sign of the forgiveness of sins and of the mortification of the flesh. Forgiveness is always accompanied by mortification, by the power that subdues within man the sins from which he is absolved. "When Paul says that we are washed by baptism, his meaning is, that God employs it for declaring to us that we are washed, and at the same time performs what it represents."[3] "Because baptism is the seal by which He confirms to us this benefit . . . it is worthily said to be given us for the remission of sins."[4]

Because baptism is a sign of forgiveness and mortification, it is also a sign of our separation from the world to God.

We ought not to be led away by wicked examples . . . to mix with the world. This is made evident in baptism, in which we are buried together with Christ, so that being dead to the world, and to the flesh, we may live to God. . . . The death which is set forth in baptism is an entrance into life, nor can salvation be hoped for, except we be separated from the world.[5]

This means that baptism is also a sign of adoption and renewal.

In baptism, the first thing to be considered is, that God the Father, by planting us in His Church in unmerited goodness, receives us by adoption into the number of His sons. Secondly, as we cannot have any connection with Him except by means of reconciliation, we have need of Christ to restore us to the Father's favour by His blood. Thirdly, as we are by baptism conse-

[1] *CR*, xlv, 125.
[2] *CR*, ix, 115–16.
[3] *CR*, li, 223.
[4] *CR*, xlviii, 53.
[5] *CR*, liii, 314; lv, 267–8.

crated to God, we need also the interposition of the Holy Spirit whose office is to make us new creatures.[1]

This shows that union with Christ in baptism means union with His resurrection as well as with His death. Ingrafting into the body of Christ means the gift of new life. "From the participation of His death," says Calvin, "Paul passes conveniently into the participation of life; because these two hang together in an inseparable connection; namely that the old man is to be abolished by the death of Christ; that His resurrection might restore righteousness and make us new creatures."[2]

While Calvin emphasizes the eschatological significance of baptism it has to be recognized that for him the unfolding of the resurrection aspect of the baptismal action is reserved mainly for the next world:

Let us learn that until God shall take us out of this world, we must be as pilgrims in a strange country; and that our salvation shall not be shown us until the coming of our Lord Jesus Christ, for He has become the first fruits of them that slept.[3]

The same thought is expressed by the Westminster divines, but in the *Larger Catechism* they ask the pertinent question, "How is our baptism to be improved by us?" They answer:

The needful but much neglected duty of improving our baptism is to be performed by us all our life long, especially in the time of temptation, and when we are present at the administration of it to others; by serious and thankful consideration of the nature of it, and of the ends for which Christ instituted it, the privileges and benefits conferred and sealed thereby, and our solemn vow made therein; by being humbled by our sinful defilements, our falling short of, and walking contrary to, the grace of baptism, and our engagements, by growing up to assurance of pardon of sin, and of all other blessings sealed to us in that sacrament; by drawing strength from the death and resurrection of Christ, into whom we are baptized, for the mortifying of sin, and quickening of grace; and by endeavouring to live by faith, to have our conversation in holiness and righteousness, as those that have therein given up their names to Christ; and to walk in brotherly love, as being baptized by the same Spirit into one body.[4]

What has been said in earlier chapters about Word and Sacrament, efficacy through the working of the Holy Spirit, and the Sacraments and faith, is relevant here. However, in connection with the last a

[1] CR, xlix, 318.
[2] CR, xlix, 105.
[3] CR, liv, 162–3.
[4] *Larger Catechism*, 167.

problem arises, for Calvin says of baptism, "From this sacrament we gain nothing, unless in so far as we receive in faith."[1] How is this to be reconciled with the practice of baptizing infants? For Calvin the answer to this problem is found in the fact that God is a Covenant-God. He regards the children of believers as within the covenant of grace.[2] "Let it be without controversy," he says, "that God is good and liberal to His people, that He is pleased, as a mark of His favour, to extend their privileges to the children born to them."[3] And again, "The children of the godly are born the children of the church, and they are accounted members of Christ from the womb."[4] Calvin also sees a child as a complete personality for his/her age; "Infants are renewed by the Spirit of God according to the capacity of their age, till the power which was concealed in them grows by degrees and becomes fully manifest at the proper time (*Renovari Dei Spiritu pro aetatis modulo, donec per gradus suo tempore quae in illis occulta est virtus augescat, et palam refulgeat*)."[5] In other words, God requires from a child the response of a child, and from a mature person response in harmony with his maturity.

A few remaining points may be mentioned briefly. Baptism, being a sacrament of the Word, is to be celebrated only by a "minister of the Gospel".[6] "The outward element to be used in this sacrament is water, wherewith the party is to be baptized in the name of the Father, and of the Son, and of the Holy Ghost."[7] Baptism may be by "dipping", "pouring", or "sprinkling".[8] It is to be administered to those who "actually profess faith in and obedience unto Christ", and to "the infants of one or both believing parents".[9] "The efficacy of baptism is not tied to that moment of time wherein it is administered."[10] In passing, the writer would point out that neither is the efficacy of a sermon tied to that moment wherein it is preached. Baptism is "but once to be administered to any person".[11]

Baptism in the Reformed Church is to be administered to those who

---

[1] *Institutes*, iv. 15. 15.
[2] *CR*, xlix, 412.
[3] *Institutes*, iv. 16. 15.
[4] *CR*, xlviii, 197.
[5] *CR*, xlv, 535.
[6] *WCF*, 28: 2.
[7] *Loc. cit.*
[8] *Ibid.*, 28: 3.
[9] *Ibid.*, 28: 4.
[10] *Ibid.*, 28: 6.
[11] *Ibid.*, 28: 7.

"profess their faith in Christ" and to "the infants of such as are members of the visible church".[1] Both are baptized for the same reason. The *Larger Catechism* makes this clear:

> Baptism is not to be administered to any that are out of the visible church, and so strangers from the covenant of promise, till they profess their faith in Christ, and obedience to him; but infants descended from parents, either both or but one of them professing their faith in Christ, and obedience to him, are, in that respect, within the covenant, and to be baptized.[2]

Adults are not baptized because of their profession of faith, neither are infants baptized because of their parents' faith. Both are baptized because they are "not strangers from the covenant". The basis of baptism for both infants and adults is God's covenant of grace. The foundation of baptism is the same in both cases, although the conditions of celebration differ.

The Reformed Church recognizes baptism in other churches as admission into the Church. Yet, to the writer, there is a problem here he has not seen discussed. Calvin in cases of necessity instructed parents to present their children to Roman priests for baptism where no Reformed minister was available.[3] John Knox, in answer to the question whether a man should be baptized after "he cometh to knowledge", says:

> He ought not; first, because Christ's institution . . . could not be utterly abolished by the malice of Satan, nor by the abuse of man. Secondly, because the Spirit of Christ purgeth and removeth from us all such venom as we received from their hands; and superstition maketh not the virtue of Christ's institution to be ineffectual in us.[4]

Further, the Scottish General Assembly declared in 1565:

> When children, baptized by a papist priest, or in a papist manner, come to years of understanding, they should be instructed in the doctrine of salvation . . . before they are admitted to the Lord's Table. Which if they do, they need not the external form to be reiterated; for no priest ministereth baptism without water, and the form of words, which are the principal external parts of baptism.[5]

Calvin and the Scottish Assembly approved baptism by a Roman

[1] *Shorter Catechism*, 95.
[2] *Larger Catechism*, 166.
[3] J. Milner, *History of the Church*, continued by J. Scott, 1828, iii, 401; G. W. Sprott, *op. cit.*, p. 56.
[4] J. Knox, *op. cit.*, iv, 121–2.
[5] A. Peterkin, *op. cit.*, p. 41; D. Calderwood, *op. cit.*, ii, 302.

priest when no Reformed minister was available, and also the Scottish Act shows that Roman baptism was not to be followed by another baptism. The Council of Florence, in 1439, declared:

> The minister of this sacrament is a member of the priesthood, whose duty it is to baptize; but where necessary, not only a priest or deacon, but even a layman or a woman, nay, even a pagan or a heretic, can baptize, provided only he observes the form of the Church and intends to do what the Church does.[1]

Two comments may be made here. Firstly, the problem of "conditional baptism" has been "the burden of much recent writing" within the Roman Church. As Father Michael Hurley, S.J., says:

> If ecumenism means recognizing in theory and in practice that Protestants in general though not in full communion with us are really and truly our brethren in Christ it would seem to follow that ecumenical apostolate can hardly prosper where there is indiscriminate conditional rebaptism of converts and an initial general presumption against the validity of their original baptism.[2]

This is true, but surely in the light of Reformed doctrine that baptism may be celebrated only by a Minister of the Word, and of the Florentine decree permitting administration by "even a pagan or a heretic", the Church of Rome in such cases has a far greater "presumptive general assurance" of the validity of Reformed baptisms than the Reformed Church can ever have when the position is reversed. Secondly, the Reformed Church also ought to consider this question in the light of her doctrinal standards.

This survey of the doctrine of the Reformed Church may be summarized as follows: (i) baptism is a sign of ingrafting into Christ; (ii) it is a participation in the common baptism of the Church; (iii) it is a sign of admission to the Church; (iv) of forgiveness and separation from the world; (v) of new life; (vi) of the imparting of the Holy Spirit; (vii) it has an eschatological significance; and (viii) it must be placed within the worship of the people of God.

These tenets are set forth in the various confessions and catechisms, and also in the Word proclaimed by preaching. Yet, we have to ask how far they are set out in the rites we are considering.

(i) The Scottish rite emphasizes the note of ingrafting with the re-introduction of Calvin's first question, and also in the exposition de-

---

[1] H. Denzinger, *op. cit.*, 696.
[2] *The Furrow*, 1965, pp. 87-8.

fines baptism as "a sign and seal of ingrafting into Christ", in the baptismal prayer "that, buried with Christ in baptism, he may rise with Christ into newness of life", and in the post-baptismal prayer thanksgiving is made that he has been received into the Church and sealed as Christ's. The same idea is also found in the Declaration.

The English rite also speaks in the exposition of baptism being "a sign and seal of our ingrafting into Christ", and in the post-baptismal prayer and Declaration speaks of the child being received into the Church.

The Irish rite does not use this term, but the idea underlies the reference to participation in "God's Covenant of forgiveness and redemption". In the baptismal prayer God is asked to "seal him for Thine own", and in the Declaration he is said to be a member of the holy Catholic Church.

In the rite for believers, all three in the exposition hold forth baptism as "a sign and seal of our ingrafting into Christ".

(ii) and (iii) These may be taken together. With regard to baptism being a sign of admission into the Church, all that it is necessary to say is that all these rites, for both infants and adults, contain a Declaration stating that according to Christ's commandment the baptized person is received into, not admitted to, the Church, the Irish rite for believers' baptism including also the giving of the Right Hand of Fellowship.

The oneness of the baptized with the Church, and of the Church with the baptized, is emphasized in the Scottish rite for infants by the common recitation of the Creed, and in the two Irish rites by the congregation's involvement in the vows. The Scottish and English rites also emphasize the common baptism in the post-baptismal prayer in both services. This is emphasized in the self-oblation in the baptismal prayer in both Irish rites.

Reference to the baptism of Jesus is found only in the Scottish and Irish rites. In the rite for infants, the exposition in the former states:

Holy Baptism is administered in obedience to our Lord Jesus Christ, who in the days of His flesh took upon Himself the sins of the whole world, and submitted to the Baptism of John in the river Jordan. At His Baptism, He was anointed by the Holy Spirit for His saving work, which He triumphantly accomplished in His Death, Resurrection, and Ascension.

In both Irish rites the narrative of the baptism of Jesus, St. Mark 1: 7–11, is appointed to be read.

H

(iv) and (v) These also may be taken together, forgiveness and new life. In the rite for infants, in the exposition, the Scottish form speaks of the water signifying "cleansing from sin by Christ" and that we "should walk in newness of life", and in the rite for adults that it is "a sign of the washing away of your sins . . . of your regeneration by the Holy Spirit". The baptismal prayer for infants has the petition that "he may rise with Christ into newness of life". The English rite for infants in the exposition declares baptism to be a sign and seal "of forgiveness of sins by His blood", and the baptismal prayer says: "Grant that this child now to be baptized therewith may be born again of water and the Holy Spirit." The exposition and petition are substantially the same in the rite for adults. The Irish rite in the Statement of Intention speaks of baptism of infants of believers "as a solemn act whereby their participation in God's Covenant of forgiveness and redemption in Christ is proclaimed"; and in the baptism of believers as "a sign and seal . . . of remission of sins, and regeneration by His Spirit". The petition in the baptismal prayer in the rite for infants is identical with that in the English and the *Book of Common Order*, 1940. The baptismal prayer in the Order for believers contains the petition "that he may be enabled to fulfil his vows and bring forth abundantly the fruits of righteousness".

(vi) The testimony to the imparting of the Holy Spirit is vital, and the most important factor is that all rites baptize "into the name of the Holy Spirit".

All these rites (except the English for the baptism of infants) link baptism with the day of Pentecost by reading Acts 2: 38–39. The activity of the Holy Spirit in redemption and regeneration is testified to in the epiclesis.

The Irish rite prays at the baptism of infants, "May Thy Spirit be upon him and dwell in him for ever," and further witnesses to this in the service for the baptism of believers by using the following prayer (also used in the rite for the Confirmation of Baptized Persons):

> Strengthen and confirm him, we beseech Thee, through the Holy Spirit; and daily increase in him the manifold gifts of Thy grace, the spirit of wisdom and understanding, the spirit of counsel and might, the spirit of knowledge and of the fear of the Lord; that he may be enabled to fulfil his vows and bring forth abundantly the fruits of righteousness.

(vii) All these rites set baptism within the redemptive purpose of God in Christ, but the eschatological note is not very evident in words.

The Scottish rite for infants prays that he may "be numbered with Thy saints in glory everlasting", and in the rite for adults that he may be kept "steadfast in Thy love and service to the end". The English rite in both cases prays that he may "ever remain in the number of Thy faithful" children (or people).

The Irish rite for believers in the Statement of Intention describes baptism as "a sign and seal of resurrection unto eternal life".

Here is a note that is not fully emphasized, but in its restoration it must be seen not simply as affecting the newly baptized as an individual, but as applying to the corporate body of Christ, of which the newly baptized is a member.

(viii) All these rites place the celebration of the sacrament of baptism within the public worship of the Church. This is excellent so far as it goes, especially where the Sunday Morning Service is an Ante-Communion. At the same time, baptismal rites can never express their full significance until weekly communion is the common practice, and the rite is placed within its eucharistic setting.

XI

THE CONFIRMATION RITE

THE TERM "Confirmation", used of the Laying on of hands or Unction, which had been associated or linked with baptism from the days of the early Church, on the basis of Acts 8: 14-17 and 19: 1-6, occurs first in a technical sense in canon 2 of the Council of Orange in 441,[1] but its use did not become general until the end of the century.

Before *confirmatio* (making fast) came into general use, the Western Church used the terms *signaculum* or *consignatio* (seal), *chrismatio* (anointing with unction), and *consummatio* (completion), whereas the Eastern Church used *sphragis* (seal) and *teleiosis* (completion).

Confirmation, unlike baptism, through the centuries did not remain identical with itself. Whereas in the early Church in the West the principal action was prayer with the laying on of hands, this scriptural practice gradually lost importance until it was, to all intents and purposes, replaced by chrismation and consignation with the sign of the cross. From the fifth century onwards the rite of Confirmation, in the West, began to be separated from baptism by a space of years. Further, it had been placed on the level of a Sacrament. No official date can be put on this other than that in 1179 the third Lateran Council used the term "sacrament" in a general sense, and the number seven was not officially ratified until 1439 when the Council of Florence decreed that "the sacraments of the New Law are seven". This was confirmed by Pope Eugenius IV in the Bull *Exultate Deo*.[2] Confirmation was also reserved to the bishop, and *ex opere operato* conferred grace.[3]

Bucer was the first of the Reformers to reintroduce Confirmation as a separate rite between baptism and the Lord's Supper, and he attached, to some extent, a sacramental value to it.[4] This was between the years 1534 and 1539 to meet the objections of the Anabaptists that the vows of a Christian should not be taken until maturity. He also held that

[1] C. J. Hefele, *History of the Church Councils*, ed. W. R. Clark, 1894, iii, 160.

[2] H. Denzinger, *op. cit.*, 695.

[3] *Ibid.*, 851.

[4] G. J. van de Poll, *op. cit.*, p. 99; L. Vischer, *Die Geschichte der Konfirmation*, 1958, p. 66.

those baptized in infancy should be brought up in the Christian faith, and at their Confirmation be given an opportunity of renewing their baptismal covenant and of making a public profession of faith in Jesus Christ. Bucer was only partly successful and the rite does not appear in either the 1537 or 1539 Strasbourg German liturgies. An examination of the rite[1] shows that it is really a catechetical act with public confession of faith in Christ and of submission to His Church. During the prayer there is no laying on of hands, the pastor raising his hands in blessing over the candidates as in many mediaeval pontificals.

Calvin, who was in Strasbourg during the period in which Bucer prepared Orders of Confirmation for Hesse (1539), and for Cassel (1539), does not appear to have been influenced by Bucer's efforts, for there is no such Order in either his Strasbourg or his Genevan liturgy.

Calvin says of Confirmation:

It was anciently customary for the children of Christians, after they had grown up, to appear before the bishop to fulfil that duty which was required of such adults as presented themselves for baptism. These sat among the catechumens until they were duly instructed in the mysteries of the faith, and could make a confession of it before bishop and people. The infants, therefore, who had been initiated by baptism, not having then given a confession of faith to the church, were again, towards the end of their boyhood, or on adolescence, brought forward by their parents, and were examined by the bishop in terms of the Catechism which was then in common use. In order that this act, which otherwise justly required to be grave and holy, might have more reverence and dignity, the ceremony of laying on of hands was also used. Thus a boy, on his faith being approved, was dismissed with a solemn blessing. . . . This laying on of hands, where it is done simply by way of benediction, I commend, and would like to see restored to its pure use in the present day.[2]

While this explanation of the origin of Confirmation, to say the least of it, needs demythologizing, it was the view of Luther, Melanchthon, Zwingli, and Bucer, never to mention Cranmer and Jewel. Three points, however, call for comment. Firstly, Calvin distinguishes between "unbelievers", who only require to be admitted by baptism, and "baptized children", who require additional instruction. The latter he dealt with by preparing a little catechism, entitled *The Manner*

---

[1] F. Hubert, *Die Strassburger liturgischen Ordnungen*, 1900, pp. 132–9.
[2] *Institutes*, iv. 19. 4; *CR*, iv, 1084.

of examining children before they are admitted to the Lord's Supper, 1553. Calvin's view of the action was:

> A boy of ten years of age would present himself to the Church, to make profession of faith, would be questioned on each head, and give answers to each. If he was ignorant on any point, or did not well understand it, he would be instructed. Thus, while the whole Church looked on and witnessed, he would profess the one true sincere faith with which the body of the faithful, with one accord, worship one God.[1]

Secondly, Calvin, like all the early Reformers, objected to Confirmation being called a Sacrament, maintaining that the mediaeval Church had severed from baptism its proper promises and transferred them thereto. He described the teaching that in Confirmation the Holy Spirit was given for an increase of grace and that all believers were said to be "complete Christians" after Confirmation by receiving the Holy Spirit with consignation with chrism as an insult and injury to baptism.[2] Thirdly, some scholars have tried to make Calvin's statement approving of the laying on of hands in blessing mean that he approved of the rite of Confirmation. The writer does not see how this can be maintained in view of the fact that it was not practised in Strasbourg and Geneva.

In the *Forme of Prayers*, 1556, and the *Book of Common Order*, 1564, there is no provision for such an order, neither is there any in the *Westminster Directory*, 1645. Professor Hardman describes admission to the Lord's Table in Scotland as a "formal admission".[3] Nothing could be more inaccurate. That a recognized service for admission to the Lord's Supper was held in Scotland, and that the *Book of Common Order*, 1564, was regarded as deficient in this respect, is evident from the fact that the Scottish commissioners to the Assembly of Divines at Westminster made every effort, but failed, to have regulations for such a service inserted in the *Directory*.[4]

Even before the restoration of Services for Confirmation, the universal procedure was for the young to be specially instructed in a class by the minister, dealt with privately and approved for admission by the Kirk-Session with special prayers offered on their behalf, after which their names were read to the whole congregation, who joined in prayers for God's blessing upon them.

In the eighteenth century, Confirmation services were restored in

---

[1] *Ibid.*, iv, 19, 13.   [2] *Ibid.*, iv, 19. 5, 8.
[3] O. Hardman, *A History of Christian Worship*, 1937, p. 143.
[4] G. W. Sprott, *op. cit.*, pp. 86–7; J. Moffatt, *op. cit.*, p. 125.

some of the Continental Reformed Churches. "An Order for the Confirmation of Baptismal Vows and Admission to the Lord's Table" was provided in the second edition of the *Euchologion*, 1869, with an historical introduction, although this title was not used until the third edition. In linking Confirmation and Admission to the Lord's Table, in placing the emphasis on confirmation of vows, as well as structurally, this was much influenced by the Anglican rite. Certain aspects of this have been corrected in the *Book of Common Order*, 1940, where the service is entitled "Order for the Confirmation of Baptised Persons and for their Admission to the Lord's Table". Here baptism is restored to its completeness as a rite, and while the necessary requirement of profession of faith is included it no longer dominates the concept of the service. The emphasis is more correctly not on the candidate's confirmation of vows but on God's confirmation of the candidate, and his being set apart and commissioned to the service of God. The Irish rite follows the Scottish in this approach, but the English continues to use the title in the *Euchologion*, giving rise to several anomalies. The *Book of Common Order*, 1964, of the Presbyterian Church of Canada also adopts the Scottish standpoint, as does the *Book of Common Worship* of the Church of South India. Because of an inconsistency between the title of the Service and the Statement of Intention in the English rite all three may be dealt with together, for while the title places the emphasis on confirmation of baptismal vows the intention of the service is to confirm baptism.

All three rites follow the Liturgy of the Word, and open with a Statement of Intention. In the Scottish rite it is:

Dearly beloved,—We are about to admit to the Confirmation of their Baptism, and to participation in the Lord's Supper, these persons about to be named. They have already been under special instruction in the teaching of the Church, and are now ready to profess publicly the faith into which they were baptized.
Then he shall read their names. . . .

Apart from slight verbal variations the English rite is identical.
The Irish rite differs in wording, but not in substance. It is:

We are about to admit to the Confirmation of their Baptism, and to the fellowship of the Lord's Supper N. . . . , N. . . . , and N. . . . They have been specially instructed in the teaching of the Church, approved by the Session, and are now ready to make public profession of their faith, and of their loyalty to His Church.
Hear the Word of God.

Then Ephesians 6: 10–18 is read.

In each an address is made to the catechumens, and then they are called upon to confess their faith in terms of the Apostles' Creed in the Scottish and Irish rites, but in the English the congregation may repeat the Creed along with the catechumens, following which come two questions on their "personal faith". In all three a vow requiring diligent use of the means of grace and to the service of God follows.

The vows are followed in all three rites by the Confirmation prayer. The Scottish form is:

Almighty and ever-living God, strengthen these Thy servants, we beseech Thee, with the Holy Spirit, the Comforter; and daily increase in them Thy manifold gifts of grace: the spirit of wisdom and understanding. . . .

Then, the Congregation meanwhile standing, the Minister (raising his hand in blessing over the candidates, or laying his hand on the head of each as they kneel before him) shall say;

The God of all grace, who hath called you to His eternal glory, confirm you to the end, that you may be blameless in the day of our Lord Jesus Christ.

The English form is:

Defend, O Lord, these Thy servants with Thy heavenly grace that they may continue Thine for ever, and daily increase in Thy Holy Spirit more and more, till they come to Thine everlasting Kingdom.

Then the congregation stands and the Minister (raising his hand in blessing over the Candidates, or laying his hand on the head of each as they kneel before him) says:

The very God of peace sanctify you wholly; and I pray God your whole spirit and soul and body be preserved blameless unto the coming of our Lord Jesus Christ.

God the Father, God the Son, and God the Holy Spirit bless, preserve and keep you now and for evermore. Amen.

The writer does not like the tritheistic formula, but perhaps that is only a personal prejudice. He wonders also why the term "confirm" is not used. Is it a failure to see its omission as inconsistent with the Statement of Intention?

The Irish prayer opens with the first Scottish post-confirmation prayer, and is as follows:

Almighty God, who hast founded Thy Church on earth and hast promised to preserve her to the end; we thank Thee for thy great mercy to these Thy children, and to Thy Church, to which Thou hast given the joy of receiving them into full communion. We thank Thee that by Holy Baptism they have been incorporated into the Body of Christ. We thank thee for their Christian training and for every good influence in their lives; and that Thou hast granted to them the assurance of Thy blessing and favour.

Here the Minister may raise his hand in blessing over the candidates, or lay his hand on the head of each as they kneel before him.

Confirm and strengthen them, we beseech Thee, with Thy Holy Spirit, and daily increase in them Thy manifold gifts of grace. . . .

Our Father. . . .

The Irish rite ends with the Declaration with the Right Hand of Fellowship, the Aaronic Blessing, and the Benediction.

The Scottish rite continues with the Declaration, followed by the Aaronic blessing, and two prayers, the first of which has already been quoted above as the opening to the Confirmation prayer in the Irish rite. The second is a prayer for forgiveness and worthy communion, ending with the Lord's Prayer. It continues:

The Minister, together with representatives of the Kirk-Session, may then give the right hand of welcome to the newly-received communicants: or, this may be done after the service is ended. He may also say these or like words:

Beloved in the Lord, now received into all the privileges of membership in the Church of Christ; consider well that you are indeed fellow-citizens with the saints, and of the household of God, and are built upon the foundation of the apostles and prophets, Jesus Christ Himself being the chief corner-stone; in whom also ye are builded together for an habitation of God through the Spirit.

If ye walk in the light, as He is in the light, ye have fellowship one with another.

Jesus said: If any man will come after Me, let him deny himself, and take up his cross daily, and follow Me.

To him that overcometh will I give to sit with Me in My throne, even as I also overcame, and am set down with My Father in His throne.

The service ends with a suitable psalm or hymn and the benediction.

The English rite is somewhat similar, but alters the sequence of events. The Aaronic Blessing is placed before the Declaration, after which comes the right hand of fellowship given by Minister and elders. Then the Minister may say: "Beloved in the Lord, now received . . ." as in the Scottish rite. This is followed by two prayers, which are practically identical with those in the Scottish rite, and the Lord's Prayer. The Minister may then give an address to the newly-received members, and ends with the benediction.

In conclusion, the writer makes three comments. Firstly, it appears to him better, especially if the Confirmation rite is being administered within its eucharistic setting, to conclude quickly as in the Irish rite than to continue as in the Scottish and English forms. The climax is the Declaration with the Right Hand of Fellowship, even in Ante-Communion. Secondly, the Church of Scotland uses the rite of Confirmation not only for those baptized as infants, but also for those baptized on profession of faith, as we saw in Chapter IX, whereas the Presbyterian Church in Ireland limits its use to those baptized as infants. The latter appears to him to be more consistent with the Reformed doctrine of baptism. Thirdly, the Scottish, English, and Irish rites for Confirmation are all placed in the setting of the public worship of God. Normally they follow the proclamation of the mighty acts of God either in the Sunday Morning Service, or at the Service of Preparation for the Sacrament of the Lord's Supper, a form for which, based on the Sunday Morning Service, is provided in all three Service-Books.

XII

THEOLOGY IN THE CONFIRMATION RITE

Is CONFIRMATION in the usage of the Reformed Church sufficiently administered? Answering the question, in 1926–27 (note the date), Wotherspoon says,

> While a full form with imposition of hands has in some regions survived, the general practice is that of examination followed by admission to Holy Communion. . . . In the Church of Scotland I do not think that law requires more; it is very general to follow examination and approval by public interrogatory, confession of faith, renewal of baptismal obligations, prayer for the Holy Spirit, and solemn benediction . . . *manibus extensis versus eos*; in some parishes, with actual imposition of hands. Where this is done, I believe that it can be maintained to be Confirmation which ought not to be iterated. . . . But this is not universally done, nor is it, where done, adequately prescribed or regulated, and it is, I think defective in intention, agreeing in that rather with the Anglican Preface than with early teaching on the subject. Stress is on Confirmation of vows rather than on Confirmation of the soul, and on good intention in the confirmed rather than on invocation of the Holy Spirit.[1]

Wotherspoon's criticisms are valid and should be taken to heart, but there is one point which must be clarified, namely, the child in baptism does not make vows in the Reformed rite. So what has happened is that the Church of Scotland did succeed in compiling a rite for the Baptism of the infant children of believers, and later added a Confirmation rite, but, while it drew from Reformed sources for the contents of the prayers, it was structurally modelled on the Anglican rite of Confirmation of Baptismal Vows, and this produced an anomaly.

The change in the *Book of Common Order*, 1940, referred to in Chapter XI, to "Confirmation of Baptised Persons" helps to clarify many issues, even if the rite itself is still open to criticism.

In view of the spate of works on Baptism-Confirmation in recent years, the writer can hardly be expected to produce a doctrine of Confirmation which would be acceptable to all.

[1] H. J. Wotherspoon, *op. cit.*, pp. 222–3.

Recognizing the unity in the early Church of Baptism-Confirmation-Eucharist and that they have become separated in time because of theological, historical, and pastoral pressures, he would point out that their essential underlying unity is not thereby necessarily destroyed. So, bearing in mind their essential unity and realistically facing the fact that the division exists, all he can hope to do is to set out a few guiding principles so far as the Confirmation rite is concerned:

(i) The rite should be in harmony with Catholic and Evangelical doctrine, and also with that of the Reformed Church.

(ii) Baptism should be seen as a complete rite. It is not baptism, but the baptized person, who needs to be confirmed by God, and the rite should witness to this.

(iii) A profession of faith is necessary. In the baptismal rite in the Reformed Church the vows are not taken "in the name of", but "for the sake of" the child. This does not mean that the child is not integrated into the body of Christ. "What happens in the act of baptism is clearly defined in the decisive Pauline texts 1 Cor. 12: 13 and Gal. 3: 27–28 as a setting within the Body of Christ."[1] The gift of baptism does not depend upon the individual's (whether infant's or adult's) acknowledgement of faith in Christ. The ingrafting is the act of God, who sets him within the divine Covenant of grace of the body of Christ, in whom the covenant with Abraham is fulfilled. It is Christ Himself who ingrafts or incorporates into Himself. The profession of faith is a "profession", not a "ratification". It should be seen as essential and leading up to the main purpose of the rite, namely, the confirmation of the catechumen by God in Christ through the Holy Spirit.

(iv) When we examine the terms East and West had in common in the early Church, they were "seal" (*consignatio, sphragis*) and "completion" (*consummatio, teleiosis*). The term *sphragis* was originally used of baptism and still is in the *Apostolic Constitutions* in the fourth century.[2] The term *teleiosis* is derived from the Septuagint, where it is used to denote consecration to holy office or use, and so came to be applied to baptism in the second century, and later to Ordination. In the East, baptism and confirmation remain a unity; they are not separated as in the West. Dr. Nicolas Zernov says:

Confirmation is differently understood by East and West. For the Orthodox,

[1] O. Cullmann, *Baptism in the New Testament*, 1950, p. 31.
[2] *Apostolic Constitutions*, iii. 17. Sections of this work may be earlier than A.D. 385.

Chrismation is not the renewal of baptismal vows, but lay ordination, by which the Christian receives a special grace, in his capacity of layman, to participate in the administration of all other sacraments. These are corporate actions, and both ordained ministers and Chrismated lay people are essential for their proper celebration.[1]

This statement is worthy of consideration when we remember that this too is the doctrine underlying the Roman rite, even though it is not as adequately expressed therein as it might be. Dr. Vetter says:

The "character of baptism" forms the first step in the *regale sacerdotium* of believers; the *character confirmationis* . . . extends this *regale sacerdotium* by giving the Christian through the Holy Spirit power and responsibility, not only to effect his own salvation, but also, by sharing in the priesthood of Christ, to act as His apostle in the salvation of the world.[2]

Here is the lay apostolate.

The object of the rite, therefore, is Confirmation by God and consecration in His service. Confirmation is being confirmed or strengthened (as in 1 Cor. 1: 8: "confirmed in you, so that ye are behind in no gift"; 2 Cor. 1: 21: "God confirms us unto Christ, and did anoint us, and sealed us, and gave the earnest of the Spirit in our hearts"; and Col. 2: 7: "being confirmed in the faith"). This is the object of the rite, that through the Holy Spirit the confirmed is the recipient of a gift. Through this confirmation involving ordination or consecration within the priesthood of believers the newly-confirmed is set apart to serve God in the Church and the world. To this the liturgical form must bear witness.

(v) The rite must include a prayer for the gift of the Holy Spirit.

(vi) The rite should include the laying on of hands.

(vii) The rite ought to include the giving of the Right Hand of Fellowship.

(viii) The rite should be placed in its eucharistic setting.

(ix) As Dr. R. C. Gillie says,

There are only two New Testament Sacraments. We of the Reformed Church, loyal to the New Testament, recognize no others. But we fail in complete loyalty to the Lord's mind and outlook unless we recognize, as he did, that life in one sense is one long Sacrament.[3]

[1] N. Zernov, *Eastern Christendom*, 1961, p. 250.

[2] Aquinas, *Summa Theologica*, iii, Qu. 72, A. 7; A. C. Headlam and R. Dunkerley, *op. cit.*, p. 60.

[3] R. C. Gillie, *The Minister in the Modern World*, 1923, p. 144.

Confirmation must not be raised to the status of a Sacrament, but, as is true of the Sunday Morning Service, Ordination, and other rites, it must be seen as sacramental.

Let us attempt an assessment of the Scottish, English and Irish Confirmation rites along these lines.

Without going into detail, it may be asserted that all three are in harmony with Catholic and Evangelical doctrine, and that they make provision for the laying on of hands. Also, all require a profession of faith, which leads up to the prayer of Confirmation.

We must, however, look at their witness to the aspect of "confirmation". The use of "Baptised persons" in the title in the Scottish and Irish rites emphasizes that it is the persons who are confirmed. Yet, they, as well as the English, in the Statement of Intention say: "We are about to admit to the Confirmation of their baptism. . . ." Surely, the wording should be along the following lines:

> We are about to admit to Confirmation N. . . . , N. . . . , and N. . . . , (or these persons about to be named), who, having been baptized in the days of their infancy, are now ready to profess publicly the faith into which they were baptized.

This would make it clear that it is not "vows" and not "baptism" which is confirmed, but the catechumens.

The Scottish rite prays, "The God of all grace . . . confirm you to the end . . . and the Irish, "Confirm and strengthen them, we beseech thee, with Thy Holy Spirit. . . ." The term is not used in the English rite. This is a serious omission.

When we turn to the aspect of lay-ordination or consecration of the laity, it is true that in the English rite in the vows the candidate promises to serve Him and keep His commandments all the days of his life, in the Scottish to work "for the advancement of His kingdom throughout the world", and in the Irish "for the upbuilding of His Church and the advancement of His kingdom throughout the world". Yet, none of the three mentions this aspect of the rite in the Declaration, where the whole emphasis is placed on admission to the Lord's Table. Important as this is, it should not completely dominate the Declaration. Here again the rites are defective. Admittedly, Anglican practice has been a determining influence, but it should be corrected. The Declaration might take some form like the following:

> In the name and by the authority of the Lord Jesus Christ, the great King and Head of the Church, I declare you to have been confirmed and set apart

to serve Jesus Christ in your daily vocation; in His name I admit you to the fellowship of the Lord's Table and in token thereof give you in the name of the congregation the right hand of fellowship.

All that can be said is that these Orders are all inadequate in their witness to the doctrines basic to Confirmation at this point.

All three rites in the Confirmation prayer correctly make petition for the gift of the Holy Spirit, who, as St. Paul says, "is the source of our life".[1]

"There is," as Brother Max Thurian of Taizé says, "but one sacrament of salvation in Christ and of integration into the body of Christ through the Holy Spirit unto the Day of Redemption."[2] The character of the seal, of baptism, in the Spirit is not repeated, but those who believe in Christ know they need to be strengthened in faith, illuminated in truth, and consecrated in service through the Holy Spirit. An essential in the Confirmation rite, therefore, is prayer for the renewal of the gift of the Holy Spirit.

The Confirmation rite, as the writer sees it, should be based on Baptism as complete, and centre round three focal points, (i) Profession of faith, (ii) Confirmation by God, and (iii) Reception into the full fellowship of the Church at the Lord's Table. Possibly the best summary is that in the foreword to the "Order of Service for the Reception of Baptized Persons into full Membership of the Church, commonly called Confirmation," 1950, of the Church of South India. It defines the purpose of the rite, as follows:

(1) The personal acceptance by the candidate of God's promises, and his personal dedication of himself to Christ as his Lord and Saviour.

(2) Prayer for the increase of the gift of the Holy Spirit.

(3) The reception of the candidate by the congregation into full fellowship of the Church, including especially the fellowship of the Lord's Table.

In conclusion, all three rites include the giving of the Right Hand of Fellowship, and place Confirmation in the setting of the worshipping congregation, but, as in the case of baptism, it can never completely witness to its full meaning until it is placed within the setting of the eucharistic rite.

[1] Gal. 5: 25 (New English Bible).
[2] M. Thurian, The Consecration of the Layman, 1963, p. 100.

XIII

CONCLUSION

"IT WAS not the intention of the Reformers," writes Dr. W. D. Maxwell, "to depart from the central tradition of Christendom and innovate according to mere whim or mood. Rather they counted themselves as the faithful trustees of Catholic tradition, and if they simplified the Roman Worship of their day, they did so with the intention of removing all mediaeval and sacerdotal accretions in order to achieve the simplicity and purity of the primitive rites."[1] This fact is recognized by the distinguished Anglican liturgical scholar, Professor E. C. Ratcliff, who writes, "The Puritan aim in worship was to return, not to the 'order of the ancient fathers', as the Anglican apologists claimed to have done but to the practice of the Apostles, as recorded in the New Testament."[2]

In the reformation of worship many historical and traditional elements were unfortunately, in the beginning, lost in the Reformed rite, but the modification and simplification were always in harmony with the central tradition. While the loss of some of these elements, for example, the *Sanctus*, the *Sursum corda*, and others, is to be regretted and did impoverish the rites, yet the very insistence on the centrality and unity of Word and Sacrament meant that the Reformed rites never sank to the "heavy individualism" of Lutheranism,[3] or the "Zwinglianism" of the *Book of Common Prayer*, 1552.[4] Indeed, in spite of the crudity of much in the *Savoy Liturgy* of 1661, it is possible for Professor E. C. Ratcliff to say, "Baxter's conception of the liturgical action of the Lord's Supper is nearer to the historic Western tradition than the conception which Cranmer embodied in the Communion Service of the Prayer Book of 1552."[5] The writer would have preferred him to have said "the historic Catholic tradition of the West."

[1] *JKGSB*, pp. 34-5.
[2] K. E. Kirk (ed.), *The Study of Theology*, 1939, p. 471.
[3] Y. Brilioth, *op. cit.*, p. 198.
[4] G. Dix, *op. cit.*, pp. 656-99.
[5] G. F. Nuttall and O. Chadwick, *op. cit.*, p. 123.

The liturgical revival of the past century has been gradual; many of the historic and traditional elements have been restored to their rightful place in the liturgy; and here, as in the Reformation era, the reform has been in harmony with the central tradition, and with that which is Christian and Catholic.

We have attempted in these pages to give a positive exposition of the worship of the Reformed Church, principally through references to the Scottish, English, Welsh and Irish rites as significant representatives of the Reformed tradition. Because of this expository purpose we have not compared or contrasted the Reformed rites with those of other Churches, except when this was absolute necessary. But it would be parochial to regard these rites as immutable or to fail to recognize that the Reformed Church can learn from other traditions. The quest of the Reformed Church is for the Liturgy which, being Christian, Catholic, Calvinist and Paedo-Baptist, gathers into a living whole all that has been discovered about ways of worship by the people of God. "The Liturgy," as Dr. A. Schlemmer says, "is not truly the prayer of the Church and has no substance unless it transcends time and place, that is, unless it is integrated into a tradition and unless it has an ecumenical character."[1]

Reform and Renewal of the Liturgy is necessary in every age, for the Church must ever keep her mind open to the influence of the Holy Spirit in liturgy, as well as doctrine, for only in so doing can she live worthily of the claim, *Ecclesia reformata, semper reformanda.*

Soli Deo gloria

---

[1] A. Schlemmer, *En Esprit et en Verité: le Culte dans l'Église réformée,* 1947, p. 46.

APPENDIX A

GENEALOGY OF THE *BOOK OF COMMON ORDER,*
1564

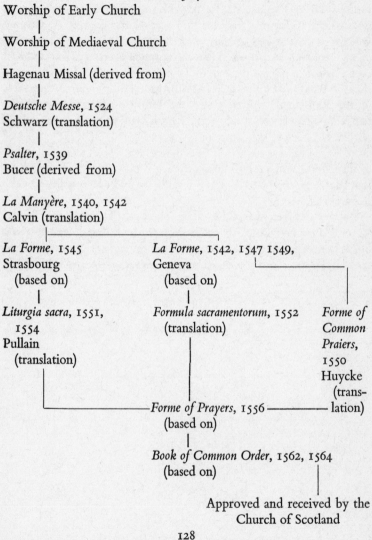

Worship of Early Church
|
Worship of Mediaeval Church
|
Hagenau Missal (derived from)
|
Deutsche Messe, 1524
Schwarz (translation)
|
Psalter, 1539
Bucer (derived from)
|
La Manyère, 1540, 1542
Calvin (translation)

La Forme, 1545   *La Forme,* 1542, 1547 1549,
Strasbourg   Geneva
  (based on)   (based on)

Liturgia sacra, 1551,   *Formula sacramentorum,* 1552   *Forme of*
  1554   (translation)   *Common*
Pullain   *Praiers,*
  (translation)   1550
                                                           Huycke
                                                            (trans-
                          Forme of Prayers, 1556 ——————— lation)
                            (based on)
                          |
                          Book of Common Order, 1562, 1564
                            (based on)

                              Approved and received by the
                                 Church of Scotland

APPENDIX B

GENEALOGY OF THE *BOOK OF COMMON ORDER,* 1940

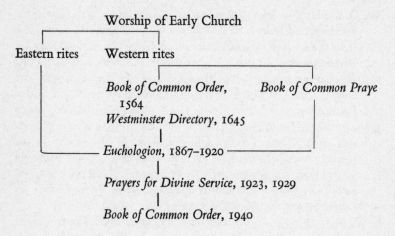

APPENDIX C

ANNOTATED TEXTS

Manuscripts:

W. D. Bailie: *The Rites of Baptism and Confirmation*, 1959. Thesis for the degree of Doctor of Philosophy in the Queen's University of Belfast. (As well as containing much historical material, see for Baptismal rites of Farel, Calvin, *Book of Common Order*, 1564, *Westminster Directory, Euchologion, Prayers for Divine Service*, and *Book of Common Order*, 1940; and Confirmation rites in *Euchologion, Prayers for Divine Service*, and *Book of Common Order*, 1940.)

J. M. Barkley: *The Eucharistic Rite in the Liturgy of the Church of Scotland*, 1949. Thesis for the degree of Doctor of Divinity in the University of Dublin. (As well as containing much historical material, see for Eucharistic rites of Bucer, Calvin, *Book of Common Order*, 1564, *Westminster Directory, Euchologion, Prayers for Divine Service*, and *Book of Common Order*, 1940.)

E. W. McNally: *The Westminster Directory*, 1958. Thesis for the degree of Doctor of Philosophy in the University of Edinburgh.

F. O. Reed: *Worship in 16th century Calvinism*, 1933. Thesis for the degree of Doctor of Philosophy in the University of Oxford. (Principally historical, but see appendices for the Baptismal rites of Bucer, Farel, and Calvin.)

Printed texts:

M. Albertz: *Kirchenbuch*, 1941.

J. Calvin: *Opera*, ed. G. Baum, E. Cunitz, and E. Reuss, 1863.

G. Farel: *La Manière et fasson quon tient es lieux que Die de sa grace a visités*, ed. G. Baum, 1859.

F. Hubert: *Die Strassburger liturgischen Ordnungen im Zeitalter der Reformation*, 1900.

T. Leishman: *The Westminster Directory*, 1868, 1901.

W. D. Maxwell: *John Knox's Genevan Service Book, 1556*, 1931.

J. Smend: *Der erste evangelische Gottesdienst in Strassburg*, 1897.

G. W. Sprott: *Book of Common Order (Knox's Liturgy)*, 1868, 1901.

G. W. Sprott: *Book of Common Order (Euchologion*, seventh edition), 1905.

INDEX